TIGER WOODS

An American Master

TIGER WOODS

An American Master

Second Edition

by Nicholas Edwards

SCHOLASTIC INC.
New York Toronto London Auckland Sydney
Mexico City New Delhi Hong Kong

Special acknowledgment to Ed Monagle

Photo Credits
cover © David Cannon/Allsport
Insert page 1: (both) David Strick/Corbis Outline; page 2: (both) David Strick/Corbis Outline; page 3: (top) © Ken Levine/Allsport, (bottom) © Gamma Liaison; page 4: (top) © David Madison/Duomo, (bottom) Sam Jones/Corbis Outline; page 5: (both) AP/Wide World; page 6: (top) © Steve Munday/Allsport, (bottom) George Lange/Corbis Outline; page 7: (top) Andrew Redington/Allsport, (bottom) David Cannon/Allsport; page 8: (top) Andy Lyons, (bottom) David Cannon/Allsport.

ISBN 0-439-27060-X

12 11 10 9 8 7 6 5 4 3 2 1   1 2 3 4 5 6/0

Printed in the U.S.A.

Reissued by Scholastic, April 2001

Contents

Prologue

The game of golf has had a long, dignified, and undeniably elite history. It has traditionally been a sport for presidents and kings, doctors and lawyers, powerful politicians and wealthy businesspeople — to say nothing of countless affluent retirees. To paraphrase the old saying, "This one *is* your grandfather's game." Golf has typically been played at exclusive country clubs, whose members were often only permitted to join if they happened to have the "right" ethnic background, religion, gender, and/or income level. It would not be an understatement to say that for most of the sport's existence, golf has been restricted to a very small segment of society.

A few years ago, if the average American had been asked to describe golf, most people instantly would have pictured middle-aged people wearing pastel polo shirts and baggy slacks, riding across perfectly manicured green grass in little carts, because actually *walking* around the course would be too strenuous. The idea of voluntarily spending time on a Sunday afternoon watching golf on television would have seemed either hilarious — or just very, very strange. Frankly, for the vast majority of the viewing public, golf had earned a reputation for being slow, action-free — and really, really *boring*.

But recently, all of that changed. Suddenly, television ratings started soaring, and tickets to PGA tournaments would sell out completely! Huge crowds jockeyed for prime viewing positions at each fairway, and sometimes the spectators would even . . . *cheer*. Out of nowhere, golf began to seem dramatic, exciting, and fun. Impossible as it may have seemed five or ten years ago, golf has undeniably become *cool*.

Now people want to read about the sport, follow it week after week on television, and learn how to play themselves.

Why has the entire atmosphere surrounding the game of golf undergone such a total transformation?

There is only one reason.

His name is Tiger Woods.

1
Growing Up

Eldrick "Tiger" Woods was born on December 30, 1975. He grew up in Cypress, California, a middle-class town about an hour southeast of Los Angeles. He lived in a pleasant, three-bedroom house with his parents, Earl and Kultida Woods.

Many people assume that Tiger is an African-American, but actually, Tiger is a genuine example of the American melting pot in action. Tiger's father, Earl, is half African-American, one-quarter Chinese, and one-quarter Native American. Tiger's mother, Kultida, who likes to be called Tida, is from Thailand. She is half-Thai, one-quarter Chinese, and one-quarter Caucasian.

As a result, Tiger identifies with all of these different cultures. Mainly, he considers himself to be both Asian-American and African-American. It always bothers him when people forget his Asian heritage, because he feels that means that his mother's side of the family isn't getting enough respect.

However, with such a mixed heritage, even Tiger has sometimes had trouble deciding exactly how to describe himself. When he was growing up, he finally came up with a term that made him comfortable.

While being interviewed on *The Oprah Winfrey Show* soon after his Masters victory in 1997, Tiger shared this name on national television.

"I'm a Cablinasian," he told Oprah with a smile. The "Ca" represents Caucasian, the "bl" means black, the "in" is for Native American, and the "Asian" combines the Thai and Chinese parts of his background. The phonetic pronunciation of Tiger's made-up ethnic description is "Kah-bli-nasian."

Tiger's father, Earl, spent twenty years in the U.S. Army. He is a former Green Beret, who reached the rank of lieutenant colonel. During the 1960s, Earl was working for the U.S. Army as a public information officer, the Army's version of a press secretary job. This was a safe military posting, far from active combat, but also rather dull. With the Vietnam War raging, Earl suddenly decided that he wanted to become a Green Beret.

Green Berets must undergo some of the most difficult and intense training of any military unit in the world. Earl was predominantly an explosives expert, but Green Berets are expected to learn many different skills. They tend to work in

4

small, self-sufficient units, and each member of the unit must be a multifaceted soldier. For example, Green Berets often receive medical and language training, in addition to learning various forms of combat. Green Berets are expected to be in top physical shape at all times. They must also be able to work independently, and as an efficient team.

During the Vietnam War, Green Berets were almost always sent to very isolated areas of the country. They were officially known as U.S. Army Special Forces, and they were sent on difficult assignments. Once they had settled in small base camps, they would serve as advisers to large units of South Vietnamese soldiers.

Because they worked together so closely and under such dangerous conditions, Green Berets often became good friends with their South Vietnamese allies. During any war, soldiers form intense bonds with one another. They share so many life and death experiences that many of them become even closer than brothers and sisters. Tiger's father, Earl, who served two year-long tours in Vietnam, made one particularly good friend, a South Vietnamese lieutenant colonel named Nguyen Phong.

Earl and Nguyen had many hair-raising adventures, and Nguyen saved Earl's life on more than one occasion. Earl admired Nguyen so much that he called him Tiger. Nguyen was a courageous and impressive man, and Earl felt that Tiger was the perfect nickname for him.

Unfortunately, in the confusion of the war, Earl and Nguyen ended up losing touch with each other. Earl was heartbroken when his friend disappeared, but to this day, he is sure that Nguyen is still alive. When Earl's son Eldrick was born, Earl immediately began calling him Tiger, in honor of his former friend and ally. Privately, Earl has always hoped that someday Nguyen would hear the name Tiger Woods, and know that his Green Beret friend was still thinking about him. If Nguyen *is* still alive, Earl's fondest dream is that Nguyen will track him down.

Around this time, Earl was assigned to a posting in Bangkok, Thailand. He wasn't happy about going to this new location, but when he walked into one of the Army offices one day, he met a beautiful Thai secretary. Her name was Kultida Punsawad, and Earl fell in love. His first marriage, from which he had two sons and a daughter, had ended in divorce. Earl's parents had died when he was little, so he didn't have much family. Meeting Tida was the best thing that had happened to him in a long time.

Tida was shy, but she was intrigued by this strong American soldier with the intense personality. On their first date, she brought along a chaperon! But she ended up falling in love, too. Earl and Tida got married in 1969, and she returned to the United States with him.

In 1975, their only child, a son, was born. Tida chose the name Eldrick for him, but she respected Earl's desire to honor the memory of his friend

Nguyen by calling Eldrick "Tiger." Tida had spent most of her childhood away from her family in a boarding school, and she knew that she wanted to give *her* child a more secure upbringing than she had had. She was determined that, no matter what, Tiger would always feel safe and loved.

Earl had also had a lonely childhood, and he agreed with his wife about this. Whatever Tiger needed, they would give him. The most important thing in their lives now was their son's welfare.

Earl had always been athletic. In college at Kansas State, he was the first African-American to play baseball in the Big Twelve Conference. (At the time, this division was actually called the Big Seven.) This was during the 1950s, and Earl experienced a great deal of prejudice and discrimination. His white teammates would eat in one restaurant, and he would have to go someplace else. The same thing would happen when they had to travel to away games. The team would stay at one motel; Earl would have to go off by himself. He endured these hardships bravely, but he never forgot them.

In 1976, when Earl was forty-two years old, he started playing a different sport: *golf*. He enjoyed the game, and worked hard to become a competitive player. If he had started playing the game when he was younger, *he* might have been good enough to play professionally, too. But even though it was too late to start a career as a golfer, Earl practiced constantly. One of his favorite things to do was to go out to the garage and chip balls into a net he had set up. Earl assumed that the more time he spent working on his swing, the faster his game would improve. Since he wanted to spend as much time with his son as possible, he would bring Tiger out to the garage with him every day.

Tiger was a restless and energetic baby, but from the time he was just a few months old, he loved sitting up in his metal high chair and watching his father chip golf balls into a net. Tiger could sit that way for hours, and never lose interest.

Overjoyed that he and his baby son could already share a common interest, Earl cut down a small putter, so that it would be Tiger's size. Right away, this became Tiger's favorite toy. Before Tiger could even walk, he would drag the putter with him everywhere.

Then, one day, when Tiger was ten or eleven months old, something amazing happened. He climbed out of his high chair, picked up his putter, and began hitting balls into the net. He could barely stand up, but he clearly had a natural talent for the game. By watching his father practice for hours, Tiger had absorbed the basics of a good golf swing and could imitate his father perfectly. The *really* amazing part was that he wasn't even a year old!

To their complete surprise, Earl and Tida realized that their son was a prodigy!

2
A Star in the Making

By the time Tiger was two years old, he could chip shots, tee off, and hit putts. Word of his talent had spread, and he and Earl were invited to be guests on *The Mike Douglas Show*. This was a popular talk show of the time, and Mike Douglas was known as a kind and friendly host. Today, *The Rosie O'Donnell Show* is often compared to *The Mike Douglas Show*, because the two hosts share a similar cheerful outlook. The low-pressure atmosphere of the show made this an excellent place for Tiger to make his debut as an athlete of the future.

The day Tiger and his father appeared on the show, Mike Douglas's other two guests were Bob Hope, the well-known comedian, and Jimmy Stewart, the movie star. At two years old, Tiger was in pretty good company! Bob Hope was famous around the world for being a die-hard amateur golfer, and Mike Douglas thought it would be fun for him to have a putting contest with this tiny phenomenon.

When it was time to go on, Tiger toddled confidently out onto the stage. He didn't even seem to notice the bright lights or the audience. He was wearing a bright red cap, a red-and-white shirt, khaki shorts, and tiny sneakers. He was also carrying a miniature red golf bag over his shoulder. This golf bag had been designed and handmade by his mother, Tida. She had spent many hours making this special gift for her son.

A small putting green made out of artificial turf had been set up on the stage. In front of a nationwide television audience, Tiger calmly drove a couple of balls off the green. His swing was startlingly mature. Now it was time to do some putting.

Bob Hope is a jokester, and he had a quip ready. "You, uh, you got any money?" he asked Tiger, as though they were going to bet on the contest.

Although he certainly couldn't have understood what Bob Hope meant, Tiger promptly moved his ball closer to the golf hole and tapped it in. The audience went wild, and it was clear that even at the age of two, Tiger had star power.

Even though his son was very young, Earl wanted to teach him as much as possible about golf. He wanted Tiger to have constant love and attention, and he also planned to give his son the benefit of his life experiences. If golf was what

10

Tiger wanted to learn, that was what Earl would teach him!

As it turned out, Tiger was an extremely fast learner. Earl began bringing him to the U.S. Navy Golf Course, which was located in Tiger's hometown, Cypress. When Tiger was only three years old, it is said that he shot a score of 48 while playing nine holes at the U.S. Navy facility. The rules had to be stretched a little bit by allowing Tiger to use a tee on every shot. But no matter what, it was a remarkable demonstration of talent.

That year, 1979, Tiger also entered a local pitch, putt, and drive contest. Even though he was a toddler, he had been put in the same category as ten- and eleven-year-old golfers. Everyone was stunned when Tiger beat the entire field and walked away with the first-place trophy.

When Tiger was five years old, he was invited to demonstrate his skills on the television show *That's Incredible*, which was a showcase for various novelty acts. Tiger rose to the occasion, and casually smacked balls into the audience.

While Tiger was making incredible progress with his golf game, unfortunately he was also running into a lot of prejudice. On Tiger's first day of kindergarten, a group of local boys tied him to a tree, threw rocks at him, and shouted racial slurs.

Tiger was also kicked off golf courses on more than one occasion, for no reason other than the color of his skin. For many years, golf had been an exclusively white sport, and African-Americans and other people of color traditionally had been excluded. Most country clubs refused to admit minorities or women. In fact, up until 1961, the PGA Tour enforced a Caucasians-only rule.

It wasn't until 1975 — the year Tiger was born — that the first African-American player, a man named Lee Elder, was allowed to play at The Masters. It took another fifteen years for the Augusta National Golf Club, where The Masters is held, to admit its first African-American member. Even today, many aspects of these long-held prejudices still exist in the game of golf.

But Tiger loved to play, and racial discrimination was not enough to stop him — or his father. When the U.S. Navy Golf Course in Cypress decided to ban Tiger from playing there, pretending that the reason was because he was too young, Earl simply took Tiger to play at a different club nearby.

During these formative years, Earl was trying to instill both the physical skills Tiger would need as a player, and the mental toughness, which would probably be even more important down the road. Earl especially wanted Tiger to develop what is known as a preshot routine. All experienced golfers use some form of this technique. Earl used Army terminology for the preshot routine, calling it an SOP, which is short for Standard Operating Procedure.

But, no matter what name is used, the idea is to develop a permanent pattern of behavior. If a player performs the exact same routines before every single shot, he or she is less likely to wilt under pressure. By learning to follow a precise routine, the player will automatically fall into those patterns during even the most nerve-racking tournaments.

There were several important aspects to this preshot routine. Mainly, Tiger was learning to plan ahead, instead of just swinging carelessly. Earl taught him to stand behind the ball and pick a target. After all, without deciding where he wanted the ball to go, there wouldn't be much point to taking a swing! Once Tiger decided *where* he wanted to hit the ball, he would think about the wind, the condition of the grass, and the placement of the various hazards on the course. Once he had a clear plan in his mind, he was ready to go.

Today, as a professional player, Tiger still uses the very same preshot routine his father taught him when he was three years old!

Although Tiger and his father both appear to be equally stubborn, they were able to work together productively. They loved and respected each other. Tiger didn't really enjoy the discipline of developing a preshot routine, but he did it anyway. More than anything else, he wanted to be the best golfer in the world, and he was willing to do whatever it took to achieve that goal.

Golf was the main focus of Tiger's life, but that didn't mean that school wasn't important, too. Tiger's parents were very strict when it came to things like studying. Their son might have a natural gift for golf, but they also wanted him to get a good education and be a well-rounded person.

"My parents wouldn't let me practice unless I had my homework done," Tiger told Oprah Winfrey, while guesting on her show. "That was the rule, until I entered high school. I mean, that was the *law*."

As Tiger got older, it was time to start playing competitively. He won his first major tournament when he was only eight years old! It was to be the first of his four victories at the Optimist International Golf Junior Championship.

Tiger's journey had begun.

3
The Training Continues

Golf is an extremely complex game, and it is probably a good idea to explain some of the concepts now. A golf course consists of eighteen holes, each of which is broken down into a tee box, a huge grassy fairway, and a much smaller putting green. These holes are generally several hundred yards long. (For more detailed explanations of these terms and concepts, see *Golf: The Basics* and the glossary, which are located at the back of this book.) The holes, which are each marked with a numbered flag attached to a tall pole, are on the putting greens. The point of the game is to hit the ball into each hole with the lowest possible number of strokes.

Whenever people talk about golf, words like *par*, *birdie*, and *bogey* are thrown around. For someone who doesn't follow the sport closely, these words sound like an entirely different language. Par is the number of strokes — or shots — a good player should need in order to complete the course. If the par for a course is 72, and a player finishes with only 70 strokes, then the score is two *under* par. If the player finishes in 75 strokes, his or her final score is three *over* par.

Each hole on a course is also given a par value. If a hole is a par-4 hole, that means that a good golfer would need four shots to knock the ball into the hole. If the player accomplishes this in only three shots — or one under par — he or she has scored a birdie. Tiger hit his first birdie when he was just five years old. If the player needs only two shots to finish — or two under par — that is an eagle. By contrast, if a player needs five shots to finish a par-4 hole, then he or she has scored a bogey. If the player used six shots, it would be a double bogey. If the player required seven shots to finish, it would be a *triple* bogey, and so on.

The word *bunker* refers to the sand traps on the course. When a ball is buried in the sand, it can be very hard to hit it back onto the grass! The term *water hazard* refers to the ponds that are a part of every course. Trying to avoid these hazards makes the game even more difficult.

The major types of golf clubs are woods, irons, wedges, and putters. Woods — which usually aren't made of wood — are used to hit long-distance shots. They are numbered, and the lower numbers designate the most powerful clubs. When a player tees off — or hits the ball for the first time — he or she will usually use a 1-wood. The 1-wood is also called a driver.

Irons, which are also numbered, are used for shots that require less distance. The higher the number, the lighter and shorter the club is. The wedges are used for very short shots near the putting green, and the putters are used on the green to hit the ball into the hole.

If a golfer is extremely talented — or very lucky — and manages to hit the ball into the hole with one shot, it is called a hole in one. Tiger actually scored his first hole in one when he was six years old. This was a truly stunning achievement for such a young player.

At the end of a friendly competition or a tournament, there are two different ways to decide the winner. In medal play, the player with the lowest number of total strokes wins. In match play, the player who won the most actual holes wins, no matter how many total strokes she or he used. Medal play is much more common than match play.

The American Junior Golf Association (AJGA), runs a series of tournaments, in the same way that the Professional Golfers' Association (PGA) and the Ladies Professional Golf Association (LPGA) do. The main difference is that junior players do not get paid. Once a player receives money for playing golf, he or she can no longer compete at the amateur level. Since many junior players hope to receive college scholarships, they are careful not to damage their amateur status at any point.

In order to compete in junior golf, a player has to pass through a number of stages. First, a young golfer will compete locally. This means entering club tournaments, attending clinics and camps, taking lessons, and maybe playing on the high school team. A player who is successful locally will move on to the state level. These tournaments would include the state high school finals, state qualifying tournaments for national competitions, and other state championships.

A junior player who consistently wins state tournaments will start entering national tournaments. These would include the various stops on the American Junior Golf Association circuit, the USGA Junior Championships, the U.S. Junior Amateur Championships, and the U.S. Junior World Championships, and the many large tournaments sponsored by corporations. The most important tournament for juniors is the U.S. Junior Amateur Championship. It is an indication of Tiger's brilliance that he ultimately ended up winning the U.S. Junior Amateur Championship three years in a row.

Tiger first started competing in tournaments in 1980, when he was four years old. By the time Tiger was twelve, he had collected more than two hundred trophies for his various tournament victories. The shelves in the Woods's house in Cypress were getting pretty crowded!

Earl had some very definite theories about the way the game of golf should be taught. He thought it was less intimidating for a child to learn how to putt first. After that, he let Tiger work on short chip shots, and then on slightly longer pitch shots. Once Tiger was comfortable with these three types of shots, Earl began teaching him how to drive the ball much longer distances.

All of this training sounds like a lot of work for a child. But Earl and Tida both strongly believed that it was more important for Tiger to enjoy himself than anything else. If Tiger wasn't having a good time, then they felt he shouldn't be playing at all. Since Tiger lived and breathed golf, this was never an issue.

Earl felt that the mechanical aspects of Tiger's game were very solid, and it was time for him to work on the *mental* side of the game. Tiger had been working on his swing, his putting, and many other tactics with a coach named Rudy Duran. Later on, he began to study with a teaching pro named John Anselmo. Earl was confident in both Rudy's and John's coaching abilities, so he decided to turn his attention to the psychological side of his son's game. Some people say that golf is ten percent physical ability, and ninety percent mental. No matter what the percentages are, there is no question that the ability to concentrate and focus is vital for a golf player.

Earl must also have been feeling a sense of urgency, because he had suffered a heart attack when Tiger was ten years old. After he recovered, Earl was probably even more eager to live life to the fullest and do everything possible to help his son succeed. Great athletes sometimes talk about

19

being "in the zone," and Earl wanted to help Tiger learn how to get there.

Earl's techniques are considered somewhat controversial, but he decided to put his pre-adolescent son through a sort of psychological boot camp. He wanted Tiger to become so strong mentally that he would be able to endure anything that ever came his way — on the golf course, or in his everyday life.

Earl decided to expose Tiger to as much psychological pressure as he could handle using some of the techniques he had learned as a Green Beret. Earl wanted Tiger to develop such strong powers of concentration that nothing would ever distract him while he was playing.

So, essentially, Earl began to play tricks on his son. They had agreed in advance that if Earl ever pushed too hard, Tiger could tell him that he'd had enough, and it was time to back off. While Tiger was trying to play, Earl would do things like make loud noises or sudden movements to try and distract him.

As Tiger was trying to make a difficult putt, Earl might shout or drop a golf bag or squeal the brakes on a nearby golf cart. He would whistle or shake his car keys loudly or toss a ball in front of Tiger just as he was about to swing. When Tiger learned to ignore minor distractions, Earl increased the pressure. Tiger may not have always enjoyed this training, but he definitely learned to tune out the world around him and focus completely on his game. No matter what Earl did, Tiger just ignored him and kept playing.

Today, because of those months of intense psychological training, Tiger is considered one of the most mentally tough players ever. Even when he is surrounded by a crowd of thousands, with cameras flashing everywhere and people shouting out his name, Tiger is usually able to maintain his concentration. Without his father's help, he might never have been able to do this.

Years later, Tiger was able to look back on this period of training almost fondly. "Don't forget, he's a Green Beret," Tiger told Oprah Winfrey, referring to his father. "And, you know, he's a pretty tough dog. He passed on a lot of that toughness to me."

Some children would have cracked under the weight of that pressure. By the time his father finished, Tiger just wanted to face more challenges. Instead of upsetting him, the tough training had only made him stronger.

4
Junior Achievements

One reason that Tiger was able to withstand, and even thrive under, his father's tactics, was that his mother, Tida, has a very different outlook on life. Earl is highly competitive and driven, but Tida is much more relaxed and serene. In her native Thailand, she had been raised to practice Buddhism. She continues to observe her faith, and Tiger shares many of her beliefs.

"I like Buddhism because it's a whole way of being and living," Tiger once told Gary Smith of *Sports Illustrated*. "It's based on discipline and respect and personal responsibility. I believe in Buddhism. Not every aspect, but most of it."

At a very basic level, practicing Buddhists believe in accepting life's ups and downs, and always maintaining a strong sense of inner peace. They consider suffering to be a natural part of life, and feel that accepting this truth gives a person great wisdom.

The religion also stresses values important to Tiger, such as respect and self-discipline. Tiger enjoys exploring the religious and cultural aspects of his Asian background. He wears a small gold Buddha on a chain around his neck, and has visited Buddhist temples with his mother. His maternal grandfather gave him another Buddha, formed from mother-of-pearl, and Tiger sleeps with it right near his bed.

Somehow, the combination of Tiger's parents' wildly differing philosophies came together perfectly in Tiger. He has been able to learn how to combine a killer instinct with respect for others. He has also developed a very strong sense of himself and his place in the world. He carefully absorbed the lessons both his parents taught him.

And yet, despite his parents' strong influence, Tiger's own desire to succeed is probably more powerful than anything else in his life. As a six-year-old, he was already listening to inspirational cassettes. He wrote some of the thoughts from the tapes down on paper, and tacked them on the wall of his bedroom. These papers said things like, "I can do it all myself!" and "I focus and give it my all!" Tiger looked at these sayings every day to remind himself of what he needed to do to become a better golfer, and a better person.

Over the years, Tida had always been concerned about her son's temper. Whenever Tiger didn't play as well as he thought he should have, he would get very upset. Tida didn't think that this was a healthy way to go through life, so she helped Tiger learn ways to handle his frustration. She did not want her son to cause the sort of commotions John McEnroe used to create on the tennis court. If Tiger got angry while he was playing, Tida would simply assign extra strokes to his score as a penalty. Whenever that happened, Tiger realized that he would have to learn how to be a good sport.

Earl and Tida also continued to make sure that Tiger wasn't under too much pressure. In the end, golf is a *game,* and they wanted their son to remember to enjoy himself. After all, games are supposed to be fun.

In the world of big-time sports, there are lots of people who work as sports psychologists. These psychologists help athletes learn special coping mechanisms for the unique challenges they experience. Tiger worked with a man named Jay Brunza, who helped him refine the mental side of his game. Among other things, he taught Tiger a form of self-hypnotism. Tiger found this very comforting, and still uses many of these techniques today.

Jay was very impressed by how calm and confident Tiger was when he was playing. A golfer who falls to pieces every time he makes a bad shot is not going to last very long in the sport. Tiger had to teach himself to keep his cool, no matter what. Once again, Earl's unconventional methods were coming in handy. During tournaments, Tiger was able to concentrate fully on each individual shot, and then to move on to the next one, without worrying about the past.

A world-class athlete is very different from a person who plays sports just for relaxation. An athlete like Tiger needs to have a strong drive to succeed and the ability to "go for it," no matter what. Giving in to the fear of failure ruins the careers of many talented athletes. Once a golfer starts worrying about making a mistake, the player will get so cautious that he or she will make even *more* mistakes. To win, an athlete needs to let go of fear and self-doubt.

Tiger knew that the only way to achieve greatness as a player would be to take risks. If he played it safe on the golf course, he would never become the top athlete he wanted to be. He had been born with a certain amount of physical ability, but that would only take him part of the way. To rise to the level of the most elite players in the world, Tiger knew that he would have to rely on his own inner strength and powers of concentration.

It is a simple reality of golf that no one wins *every* match. Tiger hated to lose, but if he did, he would try to analyze the mistakes he had made on the course. That way, he would become an even better player.

Once he entered junior high, Tiger began to play in more tournaments. Earl retired from his job at the McDonnell-Douglas Corporation so that he would be able to travel with his son full-time. The junior golf circuit sponsors tournaments all over the world. Tiger played at courses throughout the United States, as well as in France, Mexico, Canada, and his mother's native Thailand.

The year Tiger was thirteen, 1989, he was invited to play in the Insurance Youth Golf Classic National. Savvy golf fans refer to this tournament as the Big I. This is an exciting national tournament, because amateurs get to compete against professionals. For the first time, Tiger would be able to see how good he *really* was.

Tiger was still studying with the same golf teaching pro, John Anselmo. John had worked very hard to help Tiger refine his game, but even he couldn't believe what an incredible student Tiger was. Playing the Big I would be a good test for him.

Tiger beat eight of the professional players in the tournament, and during one round, he was paired up against the PGA player John Daly, who later became one of the most well-known players in the PGA. Tiger came close to beating the future star, but Daly pulled out the match on the last few holes. Even so, Tiger lost by only two strokes. Tiger might only have been in junior high school, but Daly had to play his best game to win. By the time the tournament was over, Tiger had placed second among the other juniors.

In 1990, when Tiger was fourteen, he won the Optimist International Golf Junior Championship for the fifth time. He was also the youngest player ever to win the Insurance Youth Golf Classic National. Tiger came in second in the PGA National Junior Championship, and placed third at the U.S. Junior National Championship. These were all excellent results, but Tiger wasn't satisfied. He wanted to win every single tournament he played!

In 1991, as a fifteen-year-old, Tiger posted an even stronger record. He won eight important tournaments, and was selected as the American Junior Golf Association's Player of the Year. For the second year in a row, he was chosen as the Southern California Player of the Year, and he also made the First Team, on the Rolex Junior, All-American list.

Golf observers were beginning to notice this skinny teenager from Cypress, California, and agencies like the International Management Group (IMG) were already trying to woo him. Tiger was flattered by all of this attention, but he had no intention of becoming a professional until he had won *all* of the big amateur championships.

During Tiger's junior career, he set a new record by winning *six* Junior World Amateur titles. The previous record had been four. As fast as someone else could set a record, Tiger would come along and break it. During the long, hot summer of 1991, Tiger won tournament after tournament. But it wasn't until one July day in Florida that Tiger really made his mark.

5
Taking Giant Steps

Winning the U.S. Junior Amateur Championship had been a goal of Tiger's for years. It was the most important title a junior player could win. Tiger cruised effortlessly through the early rounds, and decided that he would easily sweep the tournament.

What Tiger had forgotten is that overconfidence is never a good idea. His opponent in the finals was a player named Brad Zwetschke. Brad wasn't very well known, and Tiger expected to beat him with no trouble. But, to Tiger's surprise, he started getting so nervous that he couldn't concentrate as well as usual. He had been *sure* that he was going to win, and now the championship was slipping away.

The match was very close, right up until the end. After the eighteenth hole, the score was tied.

Tiger and Brad would have to go into what is called a sudden death play-off. In this type of tiebreaker, the two players play one hole at a time until one of them wins a hole. The winner of that hole wins the entire tournament!

Both players were probably tense, because neither of them did a very good job on the first sudden death hole. Brad went first, and ended up with a double bogey. Tiger came up with a bogey, and the championship was his! At only fifteen years old, he was the youngest player ever to win the title.

The winner of the U.S. Junior Amateur Championship gets to play in the U.S. Amateur Championship. Players in this tournament can be any age, and it is much more competitive than any tournament at the junior level. Tiger didn't do very well, but it was exciting to see a glimpse of his future. He vowed that one day, he would *win* the U.S. Amateur Championship.

Shortly afterward, Tiger got an even bigger invitation. PGA tournaments have a policy called exemptions. The committee that runs each tournament is allowed to make an occasional exception and invite a particularly worthy player to enter their tournament draw. Only the top juniors and amateurs can ever hope to receive this kind of opportunity, and even then, it doesn't happen often.

Each year, a PGA Tour event called the Nissan Open was held at the Riviera Country Club in Los Angeles. It was very unusual for an amateur to be allowed to participate, but although he had just turned sixteen, Tiger wasn't the average amateur. He eagerly agreed to play, and by doing so, became the youngest person in the history of the PGA who had ever played in a professional tournament event.

The fact that the Nissan Open was held so close to his hometown made the whole thing seem even more exciting. Usually, Tiger had to travel thousands of miles to participate in tournaments. This time, he would be in more familiar territory, and his parents and friends would be there to watch him every step of the way.

After getting permission to skip school for the day, Tiger got ready to play in his first professional tournament. Naturally, he had the jitters, and it affected his game. The way a professional tournament works is that many players have to go through what are called qualifying rounds. Only the players who finish at the top make the cut, and are allowed to compete in the actual tournament.

The Nissan Open drew a very large crowd, and Tiger found it hard to adjust to playing in front of so many people. For one thing, it was *noisy*. He wasn't used to playing on television either, so the cameras intimidated him a little. More often than not, his tee-off shots went wild, and his game was much more uneven than usual. On top of that, he had sprained a muscle in his back, so it was hard for him to swing freely. Tiger did his best, but he fell short by a disappointing six strokes. Maybe he hadn't made the cut on his first try, but there would always be a next time.

"It was a learning experience," he told John Garrity of *Sports Illustrated*. "And I learned that I'm not that good. I've got a lot of growing to do, both physically and mentally. But I'll play these guys again — eventually."

The professionals in the tournament had been impressed by the young athlete's abilities, even though he didn't make the cut. After seeing him in action, most of them realized that they probably *would* be playing against him again. Tiger was one of the most talented young players anyone had ever seen.

All Tiger knew for sure was that, win or lose, he had had the time of his life!

The summer of 1992, Tiger went to the U.S. Junior Amateur Championship as the reigning champion. He had been playing so many tournaments over the last few months that he must have been tired. Constant travel is grueling. When the pressure of high-stakes golf is added to the mix, even the strongest players are prone to exhaustion. Technically, Tiger was on his summer vacation — but so far, it hadn't been very relaxing.

Compared to playing in the PGA's Nissan Open, though, junior competition was less demanding. On the professional tour, *every* player is excellent. In the junior game, players were much more inconsistent. Tiger could afford to miss a few shots, here and there.

The tournament was held in Massachusetts that year, and a huge number of fans attended. Normally, crowds at junior tournaments are pretty thin, but this time, the course was packed. Most of these fans had come specifically to see Tiger play. They had read about this young prodigy in magazines, and wanted to see how good he was. This put extra pressure on Tiger, but after so many years of learning to maintain his concentration, he was able to rise above it.

Tiger made short work of each of his opponents in the first few rounds. The fact that no other golfer had ever won two U.S. Junior Amateur Championships in a row did not discourage him at all. He had broken golf records before, and he would be happy to do it again!

In the finals, he played against a talented golfer named Mark Wilson. Mark broke out to an early lead, but Tiger never gave up. Hole after hole, he kept the pressure on. Finally, Mark cracked under the strain. Tiger won two out of the last three holes, and the match was over.

He had won the U.S. Junior Amateur Championship for the second year in a row!

6
Keeping Balance

Although Tiger spent a lot of time each year traveling to different tournaments, he still wanted to be a normal teenager. He was a student at Western High School in Anaheim, California, where he got good grades. Naturally, Tiger was a member of the school golf team, but he also ran on the track team. The school nickname was the Pioneers.

When he wasn't on the golf course, Tiger loved playing video games, listening to music, and hanging out with his two best friends, Bryon Bell and Jerry Chang. Tiger's father, Earl, is a big jazz fan, and he had always hoped that Tiger would enjoy the same music he did. While Tiger thought jazz was okay, he preferred rap music and R & B. His parents couldn't stand rap, and often wished that he would listen to something — *anything!* — else.

Like most people his age, Tiger also enjoyed doing things like going to the beach and riding his bicycle. He and his friends went to lots of movies, and ate at places like McDonald's and Taco Bell constantly. Tiger's life *definitely* changed for the better once he got his driver's license. His father, Earl, gave him his old blue Toyota Supra, and Tiger put a lot of new miles on the car.

When he was traveling around to different tournaments, Tiger was often homesick. He loved having his father along with him, but he missed seeing his friends. Junior competitions also didn't seem as interesting anymore. The novelty had worn off. He had been invited to play in the Nissan Open again, and he had also been asked to go to the Honda Classic and the GTE Byron Nelson Classic. Now that he knew what it was like to play at PGA Tour events, everything else seemed like a letdown.

Tiger had hoped to turn in a better performance at his second Nissan Open, but once again, he didn't make the cut. At the Honda Classic in Coral Springs, Florida, the tournament officials invited a group of famous football players to play a practice round with Tiger. This group included stars like Dan Marino, Phil Simms, and John Elway. Tiger also played rounds with PGA stars like Brad Faxon and Billy Andrade. This time, he also fell short of making the cut by a few strokes, but he still had a great time at the tournament.

Playing with the pros made him hunger for the

day when he would be playing regularly on the PGA Tour. He knew that day would come soon, and he was starting to get impatient. It couldn't be soon enough for him!

Nevertheless, Tiger kept winning at the junior level, including his third consecutive U.S. Junior Amateur Championship. Since he had been the first player to win two consecutive U.S. Junior Amateur Championships obviously he was also the first person to win *three* in a row.

The U.S. Junior Amateur Championship was held in Portland, Oregon, in 1993. By doing so much traveling, Tiger was really wearing himself out. Before the championship, he had been diagnosed with a bad case of mononucleosis. But he slogged through the early rounds, and made it to the semifinals without much trouble.

His opponent in the semifinals was a player named Ted Oh. Ted was also from California, and Tiger's high school team had played against Ted's team more than once. Ted was a little bit younger than Tiger, but he was considered an up-and-coming star. Even though he was tired, Tiger rose to the occasion and beat Ted handily.

In the finals, he was to play against Ryan Armour. He had also beaten Ryan in the past, and was determined to do so again. Ryan was equally determined not to let him.

As they moved from hole to hole, the lead changed over and over. First Tiger would be ahead, and then Ryan would rally. On the next hole, their positions would be reversed, and they would start all over again.

After sixteen holes, Ryan had a two-hole lead and was starting to get very excited. He might actually beat Tiger Woods!

Tiger knew that it was now or never. If he didn't pull out the seventeenth and eighteenth holes, his reign as the U.S. Junior Amateur Champion would be over. So he took a deep breath and prepared to play the best two holes of his life.

Ryan played the holes safely, but cautiously. With a two-hole lead, he didn't want to take any chances. Tiger did not have that luxury. When Ryan made his first putt, Tiger had to respond with a dramatic shot, or it was all over.

A crowd of several thousand was watching, but Tiger didn't even notice them. He needed to make a birdie to stay in the match, and that was the only thing on his mind. He gritted his teeth, focused his mind — and made the shot.

Now there was only one hole left. Tiger had to come up with another birdie to keep his title. Even though he landed in a bunker on the way, he still came up with the shot he needed, and the score was tied.

It was time for a sudden death play-off hole, winner take all. By now, Ryan was demoralized by having watched his two-hole lead disappear. He played the hole tentatively, and ended up with a bogey. Ryan's chance to dethrone the reigning U.S. Junior Amateur Champion was fading away right before his eyes, and he was heartbroken.

On the other hand, after making two clutch birdies, Tiger's confidence had returned. Nothing could stop him now! He easily shot par on the play-off hole, and he became the U.S. Junior Amateur Champion for the third year in a row.

This was such an emotional victory that Tiger couldn't help bursting into tears right there on the eighteenth green. His father ran out to hug him, and they stood on the green together for a long time. Earl was bursting with pride over his son's accomplishment, and he wept, too.

"It was the most amazing comeback of my career," Tiger said to Tim Crothers of *Sports Illustrated* later on. "I had to play the best two holes of my life, and I did it."

Winning his third U.S. Junior Amateur Championship in such a dramatic way was something that Tiger would never forget.

7
The Stakes Get Higher

Now it was time for Tiger to take his golf game to another level. Earl decided to ask Butch Harmon, who was a famous coach for touring professionals, if he would be willing to start working with Tiger. Butch lived on the other side of the country in Florida, but he and Tiger hit it off right away. Butch had also served in Vietnam, so he and Earl had something in common, too.

Butch had coached many different professional players over the years, but he was best known for the time he had spent working with Greg Norman. Greg Norman is a legendary player, and if Butch had been able to help *him*, Earl figured that he could probably work miracles for Tiger.

Tiger and Butch spent a couple of days together, playing a few rounds, while they talked about golf in general, and Tiger's game in particular. Butch felt that there was some room for improvement in a number of Tiger's techniques, and he gave him some pieces of advice about how to improve his overall game. Butch paid particular attention to Tiger's swing on long-distance shots. For years, Tiger had had some trouble controlling his drives, and so he listened eagerly to everything Butch had to say. Butch also thought that Tiger could improve his techniques on bunker shots, and maybe learn a few new varieties of chips and pitches, too.

Tiger thought Butch's advice was extremely helpful, as well as logical, and he immediately began making some changes. Unfortunately, since they lived so far away from each other, it wasn't really practical for Butch to become Tiger's full-time coach. As a compromise, he offered to work with Tiger long-distance. If Tiger would send him videotapes of his latest matches every month or so, Butch would study the tapes and analyze everything that he was doing. Then he would make suggestions about ways Tiger could improve.

This system worked pretty well, and Tiger spent many hours on the phone with his new mentor. Butch was happy to give him the time, because he knew that Tiger was a genuinely gifted player, with unlimited potential. Anything he could do to help Tiger improve would be time well spent.

This is probably a good place to discuss some of the specific strengths and weaknesses of Tiger's game. Obviously, he is one of the best players anyone could ever imagine, but even Tiger isn't perfect!

Since Tiger had started working on his swing before he was even a year old, he had developed a very simple and smooth technique. When evaluating a player's ability, one thing golf professionals look for is how "clean" the player's swing is. Having a clean swing means that the player doesn't make any unnecessary motions or have any visible hitches or jerks in the swing. As a rule, the more simple a swing is, the *better* it is.

On the whole, Tiger's swing is considered a model of perfection, compared to most golfers in the world. He has excellent posture and lines up at a perfect right angle to the ball. Butch suggested that he widen his stance a bit for extra stability. Tiger now stands with his feet placed slightly farther apart than the width of his shoulders, and it feels much sturdier when he swings.

Tiger's father had already stressed the importance of balance and rhythm in Tiger's swing. If a player is off balance at the moment of contact, or his or her tempo is off, the shot will be off, too. Tiger swings *hard*, but he is careful not to lose his balance at any point during the process.

When Tiger starts his backswing, he lets his shoulders turn significantly, but he keeps his hips fairly stationary. That way, when he uncoils his body, the twisting motion helps him explode into action. He doesn't move his hands or wrists much, preferring to let his shoulders and hips do most of the work. As a rule, athletes can usually generate much more power from their torsos than they can from their arms and legs. Once Tiger has hit the ball, he completely follows through on the swing. His arms end up fully extended as the ball sails off into the distance.

Tiger always does two more very important things when he goes into his swing. First, he keeps his entire body calm and relaxed. He knows that if he tenses his muscles, his swing will be less smooth. And finally, he *never* takes his eyes off the ball. Beginning golfers are often so busy looking at the spot where they want the ball to go, that they forget to watch the ball itself. As a result, they won't hit it squarely and they will have very little control. Tiger avoids this problem by just keeping his head down, his eyes open, and paying attention to what he is trying to do.

Years ago, there was a famous movie star named Spencer Tracy, who most people thought was the best actor they had ever seen. He would give brilliant performances, but it always looked completely effortless. When people would ask him what his secret was, Spencer would just shrug and say, "Learn your lines and don't bump into the furniture." In other words, Spencer just tried to keep things simple. This philosophy actually applies quite well to Tiger. He has spent so many years working on the fundamentals of his game that playing golf is second nature to him. From his preshot routine to his actual swing, Tiger's body has memorized every move he will ever need to make on the golf course. As a result, he doesn't have to worry about *how* to play. Instead, Tiger can just let his instincts take over.

One of Tiger's greatest gifts as a golfer is his imagination. He is able to come up with creative ways to make shots, and once he has the idea in his mind, he is able to execute those shots. Some players like to close their eyes and spend time visualizing a successful shot before they do anything else. Tiger has found that he is better off when he keeps his mind as clear as possible. It might sound strange, but often the worst thing an elite athlete can do is think too much. Playing by instinct is usually much more successful. Tiger knows that his body knows how to play, so he tries to shut his mind off and let his body do the work.

Tiger can hit the ball farther than almost any other golfer in the world. He can easily drive the ball well over three hundred yards at a time. This is even more impressive when you consider the fact that the driver Tiger uses is only forty-three inches long. That is an inch shorter than the size most other serious players prefer. With a longer driver, Tiger could probably add a few extra yards to his drives, but he is more comfortable with the smaller size. Probably the old "if it isn't broken, don't fix it" theory would apply here.

Once, when someone measured the speed of his club head at the moment before impact, they found out that Tiger's golf club was going at the incredible rate of 122 miles an hour! With that kind of speed, it is easy to get a lot of power into your drive.

Tiger is a very solid putter, and his chips and pitches are also superb. Butch has been helping him improve his bunker shots, and will continue to do so. Probably the only area of Tiger's game that could always use some improvement is his course management. In other words, sometimes Tiger makes the wrong choice about what club to use, or where to put his shots. This is more likely to happen to him when he is playing on an unfamiliar golf course. As Tiger gains more experience, his shot selections and other playing choices will only get better. Even now, most of his choices are excellent, but this is an aspect of golf where *every* player has room for improvement.

After Tiger's third U.S. Junior Amateur Championship, he was a senior in high school, preparing for college. Ever since he had started making a name for himself at junior tournaments, Tiger had been contacted by lots of college coaches. Schools all over the country were hoping to entice him to come and participate in their golf programs. As the top junior golfer in the country, he could pretty much pick and choose when it came to getting a full athletic scholarship. Now he just had to make up his mind about where he wanted to go.

In the end, Tiger picked Stanford University. He liked the golf coach, Wally Goodwin, and his parents knew their son would get a good education at such a prestigious university. Tiger wanted to major in accounting and business, and Stanford's economics department was happy to accommodate him.

Once Tiger's decision was made, he was ready to concentrate on enjoying his senior year. He already had a daunting list of tournaments scheduled for the summer of 1994, but for the moment, being the top golf prospect in the country could wait.

Right now, all Tiger wanted to do was finish high school.

8
College Days

Over the next few months, Tiger was invited to play in all sorts of different tournaments. He accepted several PGA invitations, and also traveled to Thailand to play in the Johnny Walker Asian Classic. This was only an exhibition, but many of the top professional players in the world were planning to attend. Tiger liked having a chance to spend time in his mother's native country, as well as having the opportunity to visit various relatives.

While Tiger enjoyed all of this, his top priority was to get ready for the U.S. Amateur Championship. He had placed in the top thirty-two players for the last two years in a row, but he had never come close to winning. As the reigning U.S. Junior Amateur, Tiger was automatically allowed to compete in the U.S. Amateur Championship.

As an amateur player, Tiger had only two goals left. One goal was to become the NCAA champion, which meant that he would be the number-one college player in the country. The other goal was to win the U.S. Amateur Championship.

This year, the tournament was being held at the Tournament Players Club-Sawgrass Stadium course in Ponte Vedra, Florida. Tiger made it through the tournament with no trouble, until he hit the round of sixteen. The round of sixteen is when there are only sixteen players left from the original draw. In the quarterfinals, there are eight players left, while in the semifinals, only four players remain.

His opponent, Buddy Alexander, had won the U.S. Amateur Championship in the past, and Tiger knew that he would have his hands full. Buddy was also the golf coach at the University of Florida, and was much older and more experienced.

Buddy led the match most of the way, but then suddenly, his game started to fall apart. At first, Buddy couldn't seem to miss, but by the end of the round, he couldn't get any of his shots to fall. In the meantime, Tiger just kept his head and stayed in the match.

On the seventeenth hole, Tiger came within mere inches of having his ball roll into a water hazard. If that had happened, he would have lost.

But his ball stayed on the grass, and Tiger closed out the round with a solid victory.

Tiger had no problem in the quarterfinals, or the semifinals. Ultimately, he made it to the finals, where he faced college star Trip Kuehne. They were to play thirty-six holes, using the match-play scoring system. Trip was a terrific player, and after thirteen holes, Tiger was behind by six holes. This was a nearly insurmountable margin, and many players would have just given up. But Tiger stayed in the match. He didn't gain much ground, but he didn't lose any, either.

With nine holes left, Tiger was still down by three holes. His prospects did not look good. But then, with only three holes to go, Tiger came up with a clutch birdie. For the first time in the match, the score was tied!

Tiger gambled wildly on his next hole, sending a shot dangerously close to the water. Most players would not have had the nerve to try anything that risky. It would have been a much safer choice to take a more conservative approach. But Tiger's shot landed exactly where he had hoped, and he finished the hole with another birdie.

Now he was ahead, with just one hole left! Tiger was pumped up, but he still played the last hole perfectly. When his opponent, Trip, missed his final putt, it was all over.

Tiger was the 1994 U.S. Amateur Champion! In almost one hundred years, no player had ever been able to come back and win the tournament after being six shots behind. In addition, Tiger was also the first person of color who had ever won the championship, *and* he was the youngest winner in U.S. Amateur Championship history.

Proudly, Tiger held up the famed Havemayer Trophy for everyone nearby to see. Although he wouldn't be able to keep it, his name would be on there forever, with world-famous golfers like Jack Nicklaus, who had won the U.S. Amateur when he was nineteen — a year older than Tiger at the time of *his* victory.

"It's an amazing feeling to come from that many down to beat a great player," Tiger happily told Tom Rosaforte of *Sports Illustrated*. "It's indescribable."

Once again, Tiger had made history!

In the fall of 1994, Tiger started his freshman year at Stanford. It felt strange to live away from home for the first time, but on the whole, Tiger *loved* college. There had been one other big change in his life. Since his victory at the U.S. Amateur Championship, he was being recognized in public for the first time. Sometimes, people even asked for his autograph! But, to his relief, there were lots of *other* bright and talented students at Stanford, and he could fade into the background a little.

Initially, Tiger had signed up for five classes. His schedule became so busy that he ended up having to drop his calculus course partway through the semester. His other courses were in history, computers, golf, plus a class in Portuguese cultural perspectives.

Early on in his freshman year, Tiger joined the Sigma Chi fraternity. Immediately, he had a whole group of new friends. He also liked his new golf teammates, although he was the only freshman and sometimes felt left out. Everyone else on the team was a senior, and they all enjoyed giving Tiger a certain amount of grief.

For example, Tiger had contact lenses, but sometimes, when he was tired, he would wear his glasses. His teammate Notah Begay thought he looked hilarious and started calling him Urkel. Tiger didn't really appreciate this nickname, but he knew that Notah was only kidding. Tiger had always spent so much time playing golf on his own that it was nice to be part of a team, the Stanford Cardinal. Tiger *liked* being on the Cardinal.

Golf took up so much of Tiger's spare time that he had to work extra hard to keep up with his classes. The team traveled constantly, and Tiger often had to miss classes. During his first semester, he won two college tournaments, and came in second in three others. By the time the season was over, Stanford's golf team was ranked second in the country. The only school ahead of them was Oklahoma State, where Trip Kuehne, Tiger's friend and former opponent from the U.S. Amateur Championship, played.

Tiger had begun getting a lot of fan mail, and he was surprised to find himself getting hate mail, too. Whenever Tiger came across a letter that he thought was particularly upsetting, he would hang it on the wall, to remind himself of what he was up against.

Then, one night when he was on his way home to his dormitory, Tiger was mugged by a total stranger — who called him by his first name! The man threatened him with a knife, and then stole his watch and a gold chain. Before running away, the man punched him in the face, and then escaped. Tiger was badly shaken up by this, but he was also relieved that he hadn't gotten hurt more seriously. By sheer luck, he had not been wearing his treasured gold Buddha. This was a relief, since the robber would definitely have stolen it, too. It was disturbing not to know whether the guy robbed him because he just happened to be walking by at the wrong time, or if the thief had been waiting for *him*, in particular. Tiger decided it would be better not to give that idea very much thought.

Despite a few ups and downs, Tiger was having a successful freshman year. His team had played well, he had lots of friends, and he was getting decent grades.

As the winner of the U.S. Amateur Championship, Tiger had been invited to play at The Masters Tournament in the spring. For Tiger, even being allowed to *watch* The Masters Tournament in person would have been exciting. But this year, he was going to be part of it!

9
The Masters: Take One

The U.S. Amateur Championship winner was always allowed to stay right on the grounds at the Augusta National Golf Club, in a group of rooms that had been dubbed the Crow's Nest. These rooms weren't very fancy, but the location was certainly ideal. Tiger had brought along his friend Notah from Stanford, and of course, his father had come, too.

Tiger had a good time walking around the grounds of the famous country club. The practice facilities were amazing, and he tried everything out. He also couldn't resist taking a peek at the past champions locker room. No one was supposed to go inside without one of the traditional green jackets that were given to The Masters Champion each year. Tiger had never even *been* to

The Masters before, but he looked around the past champions club house anyway.

As part of his preparation for the tournament, Tiger had watched hours of videotapes of golfers like Jack Nicklaus playing the course. He had picked up a lot of hints that way. One thing he noticed was that the ball just seemed to zip across the putting greens. He had never seen anything quite like it, and had had to adjust his own putting as a result.

Another distinctive feature of the Augusta course was that the holes had been designed to be all fairway, with no rough areas. That meant that Tiger could just rear back and drive the ball as hard as he wanted to, without worrying about hitting into the rough, the way he normally would. Augusta National was a great course for a player who liked to make big, bold drives the way Tiger did.

During the early part of the week, Tiger got to practice with most of the top golfers on the tour. It seemed amazing that so many of his childhood heroes were now treating him as an equal. He watched his partners very closely, hoping to pick up some new tricks.

There was *one* thing about The Masters tournament that must have made Tiger uncomfortable. Very few African-American players had ever gotten to participate over the years. Great golfers like Teddy Rhodes and Charlie Sifford had been excluded in the past, on the basis of the Caucasians-only rule. Lee Elder had finally broken the color barrier in 1975, but very few golfers of color had been able to follow in his footsteps since then. Even in the late 1990s, most of the black faces seen around the club belonged to caddies and janitors.

Another problem was that The Masters was in another league when it came to press coverage. Tiger had never seen so many reporters together in one place before, and he wasn't quite sure how to handle the situation.

After the first day of the tournament, Tiger was tied for thirty-fourth place. As far as he was concerned, that wasn't exactly spectacular, but it wasn't embarrassing, either. He was especially pleased with his performance, since his back had been acting up again. He had also been fighting a severe case of nerves, and made a number of big mistakes in his shot selection. But still, Tiger thought he had recovered pretty well, and played a fairly decent round.

"It was a good start to the tournament," he said at his next press conference. "I drove the ball very well. More than anything, I kept saying, 'The game hasn't changed.'"

Following Tiger's second round, he and Earl went to visit a public golf course in another part of town. Many of the caddies from the Augusta National Golf Club had gathered there to meet him. It was the first time all week that Tiger had been surrounded by black faces, and he felt very relaxed. To make his audience happy, he put on a short exhibition, and then returned to the Crow's Nest with Earl.

The next day, Tiger's round started off well, but then things began to go wrong. He finished with a 77 for the day, which was at least seven strokes more than he had expected to score. It was frustrating. He had hit several brilliant shots, but then hurt himself with a few misguided ones.

When the tournament was over, Tiger had finished in forty-first place. He had been hoping to end up higher, because the top twenty-four players would automatically be invited to play in The Masters again the following year. As it stood, his only chance to return would be if he repeated his victory at that year's U.S. Amateur Championship.

Tiger had every intention of doing just that.

When Tiger got back to school, he was thrown right into the exhausting whirl of classes, studying, and collegiate golf tournaments. He had missed a lot of time, and he had to hustle to catch up. But it was nice to see his friends again.

Later that week, Tiger found out that the NCAA was going to suspend him briefly from the team. The amateur eligibility rules are very complex, and the NCAA felt that by being so heavily involved with The Masters, Tiger had crossed a few lines. For one thing, according to reports, they didn't like the fact that he had used a brand of golf balls that Greg Norman had recommended to him because it wasn't the same brand Stanford used.

Since Tiger knew he hadn't accepted any money, or done anything wrong, he thought that he was being treated unfairly. In fact, as nearly as he could tell, the NCAA seemed to be singling him out. To make matters worse, the university didn't seem to be taking his side in any of this.

Tiger had accepted his scholarship with the intention of staying in college until he got his degree. His plan was to turn pro as soon as he graduated. But now, after the magical week at The Masters, he was starting to have some doubts.

10
Turning Pro

As soon as the school year was over, Tiger had a hectic schedule of tournaments to play. The Masters is one of four Grand Slam tournaments on the PGA Tour. The other three are the U.S. Open, the British Open, and the PGA Championship. Tiger had been invited to play in both the U.S. Open and the British Open that year.

Although Tiger was eager to do well in both Opens, he hurt his wrist during the U.S. Open and ended up pulling out of the tournament. He was feeling very burned-out, so he was actually a little relieved to take the unplanned break.

As the summer progressed, Tiger started trying to prepare himself to defend his title at the U.S. Amateur Championship. The other tournaments he was playing were important, but the U.S. Amateur Championship was the only one that really *mattered* to him.

It had been twelve years since any other golfer had won the U.S. Amateur Championship twice in a row. Naturally, that statistic didn't bother Tiger at all. The 1995 tournament was being held in Newport, Rhode Island, and he and Earl showed up full of confidence.

Tiger won the tournament convincingly, with his final opponent, Buddy Marucci, conceding on the last hole. Although Tiger had been charged up by his dramatic victory a year earlier, in some ways, this win was more meaningful. He had played with such control and discipline that he was very proud of himself. He knew that his game was maturing rapidly. Soon, there would be no more challenges left at the amateur level.

For the most part, Tiger felt as though he was marking time during his sophomore year at Stanford. He took some interesting classes like economics and African literature, as well as a particularly interesting course on race and ethnicity, and he had a good time with his friends.

However, the NCAA was still making his life very difficult. One night, according to reports, he had supper with the great pro Arnold Palmer to discuss golf and get some career advice. Since Tiger was so much younger, Arnold automatically picked up the check. Instead of treating this as a perfectly innocent meal, the NCAA decided to suspend Tiger again. Tiger ended up sending Arnold a check to cover his half of the meal, but the whole incident was very unpleasant. A day later, the NCAA changed its mind and allowed him to rejoin the team, but Tiger was still upset.

Now he and his parents were beginning to seriously discuss the possibility of his turning pro. Earl was fed up with the NCAA, so he was all for it. Tida wanted her son to finish his education if at all possible, but she agreed that he was being treated badly.

Despite all of this controversy, the Stanford Cardinal were having a great season. This was mostly because of Tiger, who had won several tournaments so far, and appeared to be almost invincible.

He and his parents had decided that if he won the NCAA Championship, *and* his third U.S. Amateur Championship title in 1996 — which would set an all-time record for amateur golf — it would be time for him to take the plunge and turn pro.

When Tiger returned to play his second Masters Tournament that spring, by virtue of his being the defending U.S. Amateur Champion, all of the reporters wanted to know when he was going to become a professional. Tiger gave vague nonanswers to most of the questions, since *he* still wasn't completely sure what he was going to do.

With all of the confusion going on in his life, Tiger had a hard time concentrating at The Masters and this time, he didn't make the cut.

Back at Stanford, the golf team started its postseason run by winning the Pac-10 Championship.

Tiger played beautifully, coming up with a terrific 61 score in his first round. From there, the team went on to the Western Regional Championship. Tiger blew away the rest of the competition, and led his team to another victory.

He was still on a roll during the NCAA Championship, and even shot a course record of 67 during one round. On the very last day, his game got a little sloppy, but he still managed to end up in first place. Now he was the 1996 NCAA Champion, and if everything went well at the U.S. Amateur Championship, Tiger had probably played the final college tournament of his career.

Once the spring semester was over, Tiger felt as though he was under much less pressure. He played in the U.S. Open and the British Open again, and felt much more at ease this time around. He had trouble with his putting at the U.S. Open and didn't finish very well, but he came in twenty-second at the British Open. This wasn't a win, but he was starting to move closer to the top.

The 1996 U.S. Amateur Championship was scheduled to be played in August at the Pumpkin Ridge Golf Club in Portland, Oregon. Most people suspected that this would be Tiger's last tournament as an amateur, but he still hadn't made a public statement. Everywhere he went, he was forced to answer — or avoid — a barrage of questions from the media.

Tiger just wanted to pay attention to the tournament, so he made an effort to shut himself inside a mental cocoon. He had asked his good friend Bryon to act as a caddie for him, and Bryon agreed enthusiastically. Having an old friend nearby made the hoopla surrounding the tournament seem much less stressful. By the time Tiger reached the finals, he had pretty much breezed through every single match he played.

As usual, the final round would be a different story. Maybe all of the pressure was starting to get to Tiger, but early on, he seemed sluggish and clumsy with his clubs. He was playing Steve Scott, who was a student athlete at the University of Florida.

Steve wanted to win almost as much as Tiger did, and he had built up a five-hole lead after the first eighteen holes. Somehow, in big tournaments, Tiger always seemed to find himself struggling to come back after falling behind.

In typical fashion, Tiger started fighting back. He came close, but then Steve moved two holes ahead with only three to play. It was time for Tiger to reach down inside of himself and pull out a few clutch shots.

There are athletes in the world who are called "money" players. What that means is when the chips are really down, they are almost always able to deliver. Michael Jordan is the classic example of a money athlete, and Joe Montana would fall into that category, too. When the pressure rises, a money athlete wants the ball and *always* wants to play.

That afternoon, at the Pumpkin Ridge Golf Club, Tiger Woods proved that he is a money player.

Tiger was still two holes down, with three to play. He birdied the first hole, but then got a bad approach to the next. Now he had to sink an incredibly difficult forty-foot putt, or Steve Scott would be the new U.S. Amateur Champion.

The massive crowd surrounding the seventeenth hole held its collective breath. Tiger summoned up all of the mental strength that he had and sent that ball rolling right into the cup. The crowd went wild, and Tiger couldn't help punching his fist into the air, too.

He and Steve tied on the last hole, and they went into sudden death. They split the next hole, too. Then, finally, on the thirty-eighth hole of the match, Steve wasn't able to make par. It was Tiger's turn, and he was going for a birdie all the way. That shot didn't drop, but the next one did, and for the third year in a row, Tiger Woods was the U.S. Amateur Champion.

He had now accomplished everything that there was to accomplish as an amateur golfer.

It was time to move on.

11
The Decision

Right after the U.S. Amateur Championship, Tiger had made plans to play in a PGA event, the Greater Milwaukee Open. It would not be his first time at a PGA tournament, but it *would* be his first time as a member of the tour.

On August 28, 1996, Tiger held a press conference at the Brown Deer Park Golf Course, the site of the Greater Milwaukee Open. First, he read a prepared statement, during which he thanked his parents for being so supportive his whole life and helping him reach the decision to turn pro. He also thanked many of the people and organizations who had supported him over the years, including Stanford University and the American Junior Golf Association. Then after finishing his statement, Tiger agreed to answer a few questions.

"This has been both an exciting and difficult

year for me," Tiger told the crowded room. "The difficult part arose out of the need to deal with the question, should I become a professional golfer? And more importantly, *when*."

As Tiger spoke to the mob of reporters, he couldn't help being a little nervous. It made him feel better to know that his father was sitting right behind him the entire time.

"Going into the Amateur, I knew that I would make a decision — after the Amateur — should I, or shouldn't I," Tiger explained. "I knew that after I won, there was not much to achieve in amateur golf."

It was announced a few days later that Tiger had signed a forty-million dollar endorsement contract with Nike, and a deal worth at least twenty million dollars with Titleist. His agent, Hughes Norton of the International Management Group, had brokered both of these deals. Without having hit a single stroke as a professional, Tiger was already a millionaire many times over.

Now that he had joined the PGA Tour, Tiger was facing a whole new set of challenges. For the rest of 1996, he would be allowed to play in six more tournaments by virtue of the PGA exemption policy. After that, his exemptions would expire and he would be on his own. Tiger was either going to have to win a tournament or else earn enough money so that he would be ranked at least 125th or higher on the PGA's money list. If he failed to do so, Tiger would end up struggling to earn a 1997

PGA Tour card, and would probably have to attend the tour's grueling qualifying school.

But he could worry about that another day. Right now, Tiger had to concentrate on the Greater Milwaukee Open. During the first two days of the tournament, Tiger came out in a blaze of fire. He hit a 336-yard drive on his very first swing, and went on to shoot a very strong 67 to complete his first professional round.

"I thought I got off to a really good start," Tiger said at a press conference later. "I think it was a perfect start."

The following day, Tiger weighed in with a still-solid 69. He sagged a little the third day and rose to a 73, but came roaring back on the last day of the tournament to post a 68. He also made a hole in one!

After the one bad round on the third day, Tiger ended up tied for sixtieth place, but he had earned $2,544. Compared to the millions he was going to make from his endorsement deals, that might not have seemed like much, but Tiger was extremely proud of himself. For the first time in his life, he had been *paid money* to do his favorite thing in the entire world.

Tiger's next stop on the PGA Tour was the Bell Canadian Open in Oakville, Ontario, on September 8. Tiger played reasonably well, and ended up tied for eleventh place. His best round came on the final day, when he hit a 68, complete with six birdies. He also earned $37,500 for his efforts. The tournament was won by another young player named Dudley Hart. It was Hart's first PGA Tour victory, and Tiger hoped that he would be able to feel that same sense of exhilaration one day soon.

From there, it was on to the Quad City Classic in Coal Valley, Illinois, on September 15. Tiger started off the week in fine form, and came up with a stellar 64 on the second day. He was in the lead on the final day when he had a disastrous fourth hole. Tiger hit not one, but *two* balls into the water, and found himself saddled with a quadruple bogey. After that, he hit a double bogey on the seventh hole.

This was devastating, but Tiger tried to rally from the setback. He managed six birdies on the day, but could only score a 72. When the final results went up on the board, Tiger had fallen down into a tie for fifth place.

Tiger was very upset with himself, because he knew that he should have played better. He could barely *remember* the last time he had hit a quadruple bogey. Fifth place was good enough to earn him $42,150, but Tiger was still kicking himself for screwing up.

"I had a three-shot lead," he said grimly at the postround press conference. "I let it slip away, very quickly, in a heartbeat. I putted horribly."

Tiger's coach, Butch Harmon, actually thought that Tiger's erratic day would help him out in the long run. He knew that his student was good at learning from his mistakes.

That night, while eating dinner with his father, Butch, his manager Hughes, and his good buddy Bryon, he actually began to laugh about the way he had played. If he was going to make mistakes, he might as well make *big* ones.

A week later, Tiger was playing at the B.C. Open in Endicott, New York, on September 22. So far, since he had turned pro, he had played four consecutive tournaments. Life on the PGA Tour was a lot more demanding than he had ever realized.

Tiger played very well, and finished the tournament in third place. After four tournaments, he had already earned $140,000! He was now ranked 128th on the PGA money list, and if he was able to climb above 125th, he would receive his tour card for 1997. That would mean that he would be eligible for tournaments in 1997 without having to go to the dreaded qualifying school.

Following the B.C. Open, Tiger had agreed to play in the Buick Challenge in Pine Mountain, Georgia, on September 29. He was very tired, but he was also going to be the guest of honor at the Fred Haskins Award dinner to be held that same week. He was being honored as the top College Player of the Year, so he knew he had to go. Tiger had just recently purchased a house in Orlando, Florida, and he would have preferred going home and sleeping for a few days, but he had to live up to his promise.

Once they arrived in Georgia, Mike "Fluff" Cowan, Tiger's veteran caddie, noticed how exhausted Tiger seemed. He was afraid that Tiger wasn't going to be able to make it through the week.

After going through a practice round, Tiger told the tournament director that he thought he would be able to play. But a few hours later, he changed his mind. The next morning, he left the tournament and flew back home to Florida without telling anyone first.

The tournament director and the people who had organized the award dinner were all furious that Tiger had broken his word and left. A huge media controversy broke out, and Tiger suddenly found himself being attacked from every direction. Even some of the other players on the tour began criticizing him in public.

It was too late now, but Tiger had a feeling he had made a *very* serious mistake.

12
Repairing the Damage

Tiger's IMG manager and agent, Hughes Norton, moved as quickly as he could to try and stop the bad publicity. He put out a statement that said that after the stress of the last few weeks, Tiger was suffering from mental exhaustion and needed to take some time off. Hughes also assured everyone that Tiger was very sorry, and wanted to apologize to anyone he had inconvenienced.

Since Tiger had not said any of these things in person, the media still didn't let him off the hook. Skipping the tournament was one thing, but most people felt that Tiger's canceling out on the banquet in his honor was inexcusable.

Down in Orlando, Tiger was horrified by the huge outcry. As far as he was concerned, he had just been too tired to function. This was almost certainly true, because once he got some rest, he was able to look at the situation more clearly. Realizing that he had let a lot of people down, Tiger knew he was going to have to figure out some way to make amends.

Among other things, Tiger decided to write an article for *Golf World*, explaining what he had done and apologizing to everyone in sight.

"I do make mistakes," Tiger wrote. "The decision to miss the Fred Haskins Award dinner being held in my honor two weeks ago was one of them. Wow, did I get blasted for that, and for withdrawing from the Buick Challenge. . . . People tend to forget that I'm only twenty years old and this is all new to me. . . . I had reached the point where I didn't want to play. . . . I just wanted to go home and relax and get away from everybody. . . . I realize now that what I did was wrong."

Tiger also made arrangements to reschedule the dinner, and he wrote personal letters of apology to every single person who had planned to attend.

By now, he was feeling more rested and he flew to Nevada to play in the Las Vegas Invitational on October 6. It would be his fifth professional tournament, and he had no way of knowing that it was going to change his life.

Tiger shot a 70 in the first round, which didn't seem like a very promising beginning. But the next day, he came up with a blistering 63-stroke round, nine strokes under par. Several other players were having very good tournaments, and the competition was stiff. An underrated player named Ronnie Black appeared to have the best chance to win, but he was being challenged by a previous Las Vegas winner, Davis Love III, along with Fred Couples, Rick Fehr, and Dave Stockton, Jr.

Tiger was right in the thick of things, but he knew he was going to have to come out big on the final day to have any chance at all. By now, Ronnie Black had faded, but Couples and Stockton were still looking strong. In the end, though, Tiger and Davis Love III were the only two players in serious contention.

Ironically, Tiger had played practice rounds with Davis, and considered him a friend. But that didn't mean that he wasn't determined to win! Tiger finished his final round with a low score of 64 strokes. This put him in a tie with Davis.

Now, like so many other times in his short career, Tiger was going to go into a sudden death play-off with one of his opponents. Of course, by this stage of the game, he was very *good* at sudden death play-offs. He knew exactly what he needed to do.

Tiger hit a long drive down the middle of the fairway, and then sent his next shot right onto the green. Davis kept pace with him, until he sent his ball into a bunker. Tiger closed his eyes, sucked in a deep breath, and sank his putt for a score of par on the hole.

If Davis missed *his* putt, the title was Tiger's.

Davis drew his putter back and then tapped the ball toward the hole. It seemed to be right on-line, but then it rolled just past the hole at the last second.

Tiger had won!

After playing in only five tournaments as a professional, he had already picked up his first career win. With the victory, he would now receive an automatic two-year exemption for all PGA events. That meant that he could pick and choose the tournaments he wanted to play in, and would have the luxury of not worrying about trying to earn a tour card. He had also now qualified for all of the grand slam events for 1997. After only six weeks as a professional, it was hard to believe that he had already achieved so much.

A week later, on October 13, Tiger came in third in the LaCantera Texas Open in San Antonio. After that, he was heading back to Florida to play in the Disney World/Oldsmobile Golf Classic. Even though he was still reeling from his surprise victory in Las Vegas, Tiger came up with another solid four rounds. He finished with a score of twenty-one under par for the tournament, and had to wait for the players who were still on the course to finish their rounds before he would know the final standings.

A golfer named Taylor Smith had been having a great day, and it looked as though he and Tiger were going to end up in sudden death. But then, something very unusual happened. Another player complained that Taylor had been using a two-grip putter, which is illegal on the PGA Tour.

The tournament officials examined Taylor's putter, and decided to disqualify him on the spot.

Taylor was stunned by this turn of events — and so was Tiger. This was the last thing he would have anticipated. Without even having to go through a play-off, he had won yet another title! It might not have been the way he would have *chosen* to receive his second victory, but it still counted.

Tiger's next stop was The Tour Championship in Tulsa, Oklahoma, on October 28. He produced an even-par 70 in his first round, and was feeling pretty good about things. He and his family were staying together in a downtown hotel, and Tiger was feeling very relaxed. But then, that night at about three in the morning, Tiger's father woke up with chest pains. Earl was rushed to the emergency room at St. Francis Hospital, and then admitted as the victim of a possible heart attack.

Suddenly, as far as Tiger was concerned, golf was the least important thing in the world.

13
Anxious Hours

Tiger stayed up all night, keeping his parents company. In the morning, his father *insisted* that Tiger go play his round. Tiger didn't want to leave, but finally, he agreed.

He played so badly that everyone knew that something must be wrong, but no one was sure what had happened. Tiger's mind was at the hospital, and the best his body could manage was a 78 score. Under the circumstances, it was a very brave effort on his part.

As soon as he was finished, Tiger rushed right back to the hospital to be at his father's side. The doctors had not yet made a diagnosis, and Tiger and his parents were very concerned. Ten years earlier, Earl had had a heart attack, and he was also a heavy smoker. He was at high risk for any one of a number of serious conditions.

Finally, the doctors decided that Earl was suffering from pneumonia, as well as some blockages in his coronary arteries. He would have to stay in the hospital for a few days, and then fly back to California for further treatment. He would almost certainly need bypass surgery, but he would recover.

With the distraction of worrying about his father, Tiger finished the tournament tied for twenty-first place. But he was so relieved that his father was feeling better, the tournament results didn't matter at all.

"There are more important things than golf," Tiger said at the press conference after his third round. "Golf is very minuscule when it comes to your father. It was awfully hard playing, but he wanted me to come out here and do my best. I didn't want to be out here at all. Family is extremely important, it's the number-one priority in my life, and always will be."

The Tour Championship would be the last PGA tournament Tiger played in 1996. He had gone to eight different events, and come away with two victories and five top-five finishes. He had earned almost eight hundred thousand dollars in just two and a half months. For someone who was supposed to be a rookie, his record was pretty incredible.

Tiger took a few weeks off while his father recuperated, and then got back to work. During his vacation, he *did* take the time to attend the rescheduled Fred Haskins Award dinner. He still felt badly about having skipped it the first time, and wanted to make sure people knew how sorry he was.

To finish off the year, Tiger played in three non-PGA events, including the famous "Skins Game" shoot-out. In the Skins Game, he went up against Fred Couples, Tom Watson, and John Daly. He came in third, but felt like a winner, anyway.

Then, in late December, Tiger received the tremendous honor of being named the 1996 *Sports Illustrated* Sportsman of the Year. This award is given each year to the athlete *Sports Illustrated* believes represents the best combination of sportsmanship, character, and performance. Winners in previous years include stars like Michael Jordan, Chris Evert, Mary Lou Retton, and Cal Ripken, Jr. Tiger was only the fifth golfer to win the honor, and he was the first to do it since 1978, when Jack Nicklaus was chosen.

Tiger opened the 1997 golf season by going to the Mercedes Championships in Carlsbad, California. There were only thirty-one other players there, each of whom had won at least one PGA tournament the year before. Tiger had qualified because of his wins at Las Vegas and Disney World.

"I want to play well, this first full year on tour," Tiger told reporters. "I'm going to plan my schedule quarterly. I don't ever want to be as tired as I was last fall."

Apparently, Tiger was starting off 1997 feeling fresh as a daisy, because he won the tournament.

It went right down to the wire, with Tiger battling against 1996 Player of the Year Tom Lehman in sudden death. Tiger emerged with the win, and after only nine professional tournaments, he had already won more than one million dollars in prize money. That was the fastest any player had ever reached the magic seven-figure mark in the history of the PGA.

The next stop on Tiger's schedule was the Phoenix Open in Scottsdale, Arizona. He only managed to end up in a tie for eighteenth place, but even Tiger knew that he couldn't win *every* tournament.

Gigantic crowds followed him wherever he went, and Tiger was finding it difficult to adjust to being a celebrity. More than anything else, he missed having his privacy. Now he was a public figure twenty-four hours a day. If he had to be famous, though, he wanted to use that fame in a good way. At the Phoenix Open, he announced that he and his parents were forming the Tiger Woods Foundation. The foundation would be used to help inner-city children, both by promoting golf and setting up other kinds of charities.

Tiger's major role in the foundation would be to run golf clinics in various cities as he traveled on the tour. On Martin Luther King Day in Phoenix, Tiger sponsored his first teaching clinic, and more than twenty-five hundred kids attended. It seemed clear that his clinics were going to be a smashing success.

"I'm in a position to influence people in a positive way," Tiger explained to the press. "Gosh, that's a position anyone would like to be in. That's what life's all about."

After finishing up in Phoenix, Tiger was slated to play in the Pebble Beach Pro-Am. He played a celebrity round with the actor Kevin Costner, and they both had a great time.

During the actual tournament, Tiger came very close to breaking the course record of 62, but he ended up with a 63. He gave the eventual winner, Mark O'Meara, a tough battle, but lost by one stroke.

About a week later, Tiger and his mother flew to Thailand for the first of two non-PGA events. When they arrived in Bangkok in the middle of the night, at least one thousand people were waiting for them at the airport. Tiger was very tired from the flight, and a little overwhelmed by the size of the crowd.

After a couple of days, it seemed as though the entire country had embraced him as a native. If people in America thought of him as being an African-American, people in Thailand were convinced that he was Thai, through and through. The Thai government even gave him honorary citizenship.

The tournament itself was something of an anticlimax. Tiger won easily, against a rather weak field, with a final score of twenty under par for the tournament.

"It really touches my heart to have won in Thailand," Tiger told the press afterward. "I think just winning period is a great feeling, but doing something like this in a place I feel at home is special."

After their great stay in Thailand, Tiger and his mother flew on to Melbourne, Australia, for the Australian Masters. Jet-lagged and still suffering from the effects of some heat exhaustion he had experienced in Thailand, Tiger was not in top form. He did his best, but ended up in a tie for eighth place, while two Australians, Peter O'Malley and Lucas Parsons, ran away with the tournament.

Despite his below-average performance, Tiger was mobbed by fans throughout his entire visit. President Clinton was also in town, but the Australians were much more interested in seeing Tiger Woods. Whether he won or not, he was still their new American hero.

When Tiger and Tida got on the plane to fly back to the United States, Tiger couldn't help letting out a sigh of relief. It had been a very eventful trip, and he couldn't wait to get home.

Shortly after Tiger and his mother returned to California, Tiger's father underwent an already scheduled heart bypass surgery in Los Angeles. The operation went well, so Tiger decided to play in the Nissan Open in Los Angeles in February 1997. He had not wanted to commit to the tournament until he was absolutely sure that his father was going to be okay. Tiger only managed a tie for twentieth place, but once again, his father's health must have been uppermost in his mind. Therefore, his game and his concentration both seemed a little shaky.

Once his father had been discharged from the hospital, Tiger could finally relax. To prepare for the upcoming Masters, he used the Bay Hill Invitational and The Players Championship as tuneups. He didn't come close to winning either tournament, but he was more concerned about getting his swing in a good groove and getting his mind back on the serious business of golf.

The Masters was rapidly approaching. It would be Tiger's first time back as a full-fledged professional, and he wanted to play the best golf of his life.

Tiger didn't just want to win; he wanted to make history.

14
One for the Record Books

A few days before The Masters, Tiger was practicing at the club in Isleworth, his Florida home. To his own amazement, he shot a 59-stroke round. This was an unheard-of thirteen under par, and broke the previous course record by a full five strokes. If Tiger had been afraid that he wasn't ready for The Masters, his doubts had now been erased.

As one of the four major tournaments in golf, The Masters always attracts the best players in the world. Even though it was his third trip to the tournament, this time Tiger felt as though he really *belonged* there.

On Thursday, April 10, 1997, Tiger shot a decent, if not overpowering, 70 in the first round. This score left him two strokes under par, and in fourth place. Tiger was fairly happy with his results, but knew that he could do better.

In the second round, Tiger put together everything he had ever learned and shot a 66, leaving him six under par for the tournament. This was such a powerful round that at the end of the day, he found himself alone in first place with a three-stroke lead.

"That's what I came to do — to try and win the tournament," Tiger said in the press room after having taken the lead in his first major tournament as a professional. "I'm pretty proud of the way I played. I didn't force anything, I played strategic golf."

In the meantime, the rest of the players were starting to get a little uneasy. Tiger was clearly on a roll, and if they weren't careful, they would soon all be out of contention. They would have been even more nervous if they had known that shortly after his outstanding second round, Tiger went back to the practice area and ran through two bags of balls. His philosophy had always been that practice makes perfect — and he wanted to be perfect.

On Saturday, April 12, Tiger felt just as strong and confident as he had the day before. For some reason, everything in his game seemed to be coming together at the exact same time. This might be the biggest, most pressure-packed tournament of the year, but Tiger had gone into that mythical space known as the zone, and he hadn't come out yet.

In fact, during his third round, he went even *deeper* into the zone. From fellow players to tournament officials to the thousands of die-hard fans, everyone at the Augusta National Golf Club watched Tiger in complete awe. At its weakest moments, his game still seemed superhuman.

Tiger scorched his way around the course in a jaw-dropping 65 strokes. The other players seemed shell-shocked when they realized that Tiger was now nine strokes ahead and was apparently going to win The Masters without even looking back. It would be almost impossible for anyone to catch him now.

During most Masters Tournaments, the final round on Sunday is more competitive and exciting than almost anything else in the world of sports. Traditionally, the top players battle all the way to the final hole, with leads changing on every shot. Occasionally, the outcome of the tournament would be decided in sudden death, and drama was the order of the day.

This year was completely different. Tiger started out with his nine-stroke lead, and there didn't seem to be much chance that he would come away with anything other than a smashing victory.

The fans following Tiger from hole to hole, and the fans watching television all over the world, all knew that they were witnessing something special. Tiger had turned The Masters Championship into his own private showcase, and anyone who was watching felt lucky to be a witness to the scene.

Tiger practically flew through his final round, hitting towering drives and sinking perfect putts. The rest of the field had been left so far behind that they didn't even seem to exist. The Masters and Tiger Woods had become one. With a golf club in his hand, he was a poet, he was an artist, and he was a true *master*.

When it was all over, Tiger had won by a record-breaking twelve strokes. He had been calm and collected through the tournament, but as soon as he sank his final putt, the emotions that had been building up inside of him began spilling out.

He raced over to where his father and mother were waiting, and hugged them as hard as he could. It was impossible not to cry at such a moment, and all three of them did. After all the years of love and work and sacrifice, they were able to share this feeling of incredible joy. It was something they would never forget as long as they lived.

Tiger's lifelong dream of winning The Masters had finally come true, and in the process, he had changed the game of golf forever.

15
Growing Pains

During his incredible run at the 1997 Masters, Tiger had broken so many records that most people lost track. He was the youngest player ever to win The Masters, and he was the first person of color who had ever won *any* major professional golf championship. His tournament scoring total of 270 was the lowest in Masters history, and his twelve-stroke victory was the largest margin posted in any major tournament since 1862. By finishing eighteen under par, Tiger had tied the all-time low from *all* of the major tournaments that had ever been played. If Tiger had come into The Masters with a roar, he had gone out with one, too!

On top of everything else, Tiger showed extraordinary grace and charisma in his final press conference after his historic victory by giving credit to

Jackie Robinson, as well as the African-American golfers who had come before him.

"I wasn't the pioneer," he said honestly, as he spoke to the press. "Charlie Sifford, Lee Elder, Ted Rhodes — those are the guys who paved the way. All night I was thinking about them, what they've done for me, and the game of golf. Coming up eighteen, I said a little prayer of thanks to those guys. *Those* guys are the ones who did it."

After he put on his 42-long green jacket — the mark of a true champion — Tiger grinned proudly.

"I've always dreamed of playing The Masters and winning it," he said. "Everyone who is a little kid dreams of playing in The Masters and winning."

The difference between Tiger and everyone else was that most people could only *dream* about it.

In the months following his dramatic victory at The Masters, Tiger found himself in the center of a whirlwind. If he had thought that he was famous before, he knew now that he had only been warming up for the incredible onslaught of attention that was coming his way. It was a lot to handle, but fortunately, people like Michael Jordan and Ken Griffey Jr. reached out to help Tiger deal with these mind-blowing changes in his everyday life. Practically overnight, Tiger had soared to a level of fame that seems inconceivable. Tiger is also lucky to have two loving parents who have always supported and protected him, no matter what.

Although Tiger played well throughout the rest

of 1997, his astounding victory at The Masters was definitely the highlight of his year. He immediately followed that major championship with a solid victory at the Byron Nelson Classic tournament. This led to his achieving his very first number one ranking as a professional golfer, after only forty-two weeks on the Tour! No golfer in history had ever marched to the top so quickly, and at only twenty-one, Tiger was by far the youngest player to accomplish this feat.

Tiger also came away with a win at the Western Open in July, but the rest of his 1997 tournament results varied widely. He scored among the top ten finishers at three other tournaments, but finished as low as 67th place in the Memorial Tournament and did not even make the final cut at the Canadian Open. Most golfers experience a roller-coaster of winning streaks and slumps throughout their careers, and now Tiger was finding this out the hard way. He hated losing, but he knew that it was a natural part of the "fickle" sport of golf.

Tiger received another great honor when he was one of four players selected to represent the United States at the prestigious Ryder Cup competition. But to his dismay, he did not do very well in the demanding match play format. (In the Ryder Cup, matches are one-on-one, rather than being based on a total four-round score, the way it is in most professional golf tournaments. The scoring in typical PGA events is known as medal play.) In five individual matches against five of America's

European competitors, Tiger won only one, lost three, and tied once. It was a great compliment to have been invited to represent his country, but Tiger was sorry not to have been able to do more to help the rest of the team.

In the three other major tournaments following The Masters — the U.S. Open, the British Open, and the PGA Championships — Tiger finished up in nineteenth place, twenty-fourth place, and thirty-first place, respectively. There was no question that Tiger was a brilliant player, but there were also many other gifted athletes on the PGA Tour. Tiger knew that he would have to continue practicing and work to improve his game if he wanted to become the best golfer in the world someday. He was very happy when the Associated Press named him the Male Athlete of the Year for 1997, but he was ready to make 1998 even more impressive!

As the 1998 season began, the media, and the public — and maybe even Tiger himself — were still expecting him to win every single time he played. Television ratings had risen significantly since Tiger had come onto the scene. Tournament crowds were growing so large and enthusiastic that huge security forces had to be hired to keep the spectators under control whenever Tiger played. All of these fans were eager to see the new star, Tiger Woods, blow away the rest of the competition. But golf is such a challenging and unpredictable game, that *no one* would be capable of rising to that standard during every tournament. Tiger was no exception to this rule in his sophomore season.

However, Tiger did deliver the excitement everyone wanted to see at the Johnnie Walker Classic, which was a non-PGA Tour event. The reason Tiger had signed up for the tournament was because it was being played in Thailand, where his mother Kultida had been born. Tiger was proud of his Asian heritage, and wanted to play well in order to honor his Thai roots. Unfortunately, by the end of the third round on Saturday, Tiger was lagging behind leader Ernie Els by a full eight strokes! With only one round left to play, he had little or no chance of winning.

But any fan of Tiger's knows that he never gives up! On Sunday, Tiger shot a blistering 65, which was seven shots below par. But with an eight-stroke lead, he knew that his rival Ernie would beat him easily if he also played a good round that day. Ernie started the afternoon off playing well, but then his game fell apart on the back nine. By the time he had finished, he and Tiger were tied for first place! When that happens, the two players go into what is called a play-off round. Sometimes, this is based upon who gets the best combined score on a certain number of holes. Other times, it is sudden death, and whichever player plays the best on a *single* hole wins. If the players tie, the sudden death continues until one player finally outlasts the other.

On the first sudden-death play-off hole, Tiger

and Ernie matched each other with easy pars. The drama was building as they moved to their second sudden-death hole. Ernie shot first, and had a chance to sink a clutch birdie putt. But he missed by a few inches, and now it was Tiger's chance. If he made his putt, *he* would have a birdie and be the automatic winner.

Tiger studied the texture of the green surrounding the hole, and then he took a deep breath. Smoothly, he swung his club back and tapped the ball towards the hole. When it dropped inside the cup, the predominantly Thai crowd erupted into enthusiastic cheers. Tiger Woods, a player they considered their own, had won!

In the first three official PGA tournaments of 1998, Tiger was not as fortunate as he had been in Thailand. He came in second, then third, and then second again. Tiger couldn't help being frustrated about falling just barely short in three consecutive tournaments. That last defeat, which was at the Nissan Open, had been especially disappointing, because he had lost in a play-off round against Billy Mayfair. To come so close to a victory — and then lose at the last second — was hard to accept. Tiger felt that he excelled at play-offs, and it came as an unhappy surprise to lose one.

The pressure to win was especially intense at the 1998 Masters in April. Everyone expected Tiger to repeat the same dominating performance he had given the year before. Tiger played his best, but he ended up tied for eighth when the final results were posted on the leaderboard. It is considered excellent to place in the top ten at any PGA tournament, especially one of the four majors, but it was a letdown compared to his 1997 Masters tournament.

But frankly, after a year of constant media attention and fame, Tiger couldn't help feeling a little bit worn-out. There had been so many changes in his life in only twelve short months! He was now recognized constantly, and people watched every move he made whenever he was out in public. That made it very hard to perform week after week, against the best players in the world, without losing his concentration. It was also a big adjustment to play full-time on the professional tour. The unrelenting schedule was very different from playing more casually as an amateur or at the college level. In addition to playing PGA events, Tiger also spent a lot of time making charity appearances, especially through the golf clinics he sponsored through the Tiger Woods Foundation. He was happy to be able to influence younger players, but it was hard to find enough free time to relax and just enjoy himself. After all, he was still only twenty-two years old!

Finally, Tiger got his first PGA victory of the year at the BellSouth Classic. With four superb rounds, which included a sparkling 63 in the third, Tiger won with a final score that was seventeen under par. It was a relief to have finally come away with another PGA victory! Unfortunately, although he placed in the top ten in seven more events that year, the BellSouth ended up being the only sanc-

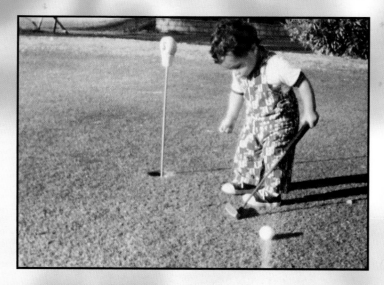

Tiger Woods on a golfing green at eleven months old.

At eighteen months, Tiger had already learned how to putt.

Three-year-old Tiger shows off his perfect form.

Tiger's trophy shelf is crowded — and he's only five years old!

Tiger at 15, with his dad, Earl, and his mom, Tida.

In 1991, at age 15, Tiger Woods became the youngest golfer to win the U.S. Junior Title.

Tiger Woods with the 1994 Stanford golf team.

Like father, like son: Tiger and his dad on the green in 1995.

Tiger Woods with
the U.S. Amateur
trophy. He
became the first
player to win
the championship
three years in
a row.

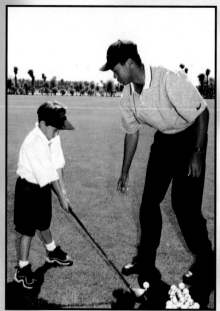

Tiger helping
a young golfer
at one of his
golf clinics.

Tiger celebrates on the eighteenth hole — he's just become the youngest golfer to win The Masters Championship! The date is April 13, 1997.

Tiger practices his swing with his dog.

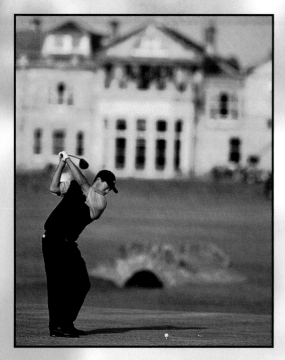

Tiger on the green at the 2000 British Open in Scotland.

A proud Tiger kisses his trophy after winning his first British Open on July 23, 2000.

Tiger swings for the moon at the 2000 PGA Championship in Louisville, Kentucky...

...and wins it all! He became the first golfer to win both the PGA Championship and the British Open in one year.

tioned tournament he won in 1998. He *did* place in the top ten at twelve different tournaments, but for someone as competitive as Tiger is, that wasn't much consolation.

Tiger's game was slowly maturing and becoming more disciplined, but even he would have agreed that his results so far had been inconsistent. Some people had begun to wonder aloud if Tiger's overwhelming performance at the 1997 Masters had been a fluke. After all, it was not uncommon in professional sports for a young prodigy to come bursting into the spotlight — and then disappear almost as quickly. Other people theorized that he had only won because the particular layout of the course at the Masters tournament in Georgia perfectly matched Tiger's special ability to hit towering drives, and that he would have trouble ever winning on other types of courses. What none of them realized was that Tiger knew *exactly* what he was doing, even when it seemed as though he was in a slump.

For Tiger, the state of his game was simple: He just wanted to become the best player he could be. With that in mind, he and his long-time coach, Butch Harmon, had been spending more than a year analyzing, refining, and trying to perfect his swing. Whenever Tiger wasn't actually competing, he was practicing. Often, he even spent hours practicing *after* he had been playing in a tournament all day.

Tiger and Coach Harmon started with the absolute basics of golf, and reworked every single aspect of Tiger's golf game — his drives, his chips, his pitch shots, his bunker shots, his putting, *everything*. They worked on his stance, his grip, his balance, his timing, his control, his accuracy, and every other imaginable facet of the sport. Tiger practiced, and studied, and then practiced some more. It is hard to believe that such a talented player would be humble enough to start over practically from scratch and work on the most elementary skills, but that is exactly what Tiger did. Sometimes, it is important to take a few steps backward and reevaluate the situation, before you can move ahead again. So Tiger hit hundreds and hundreds of balls, day after day. A player of Tiger's caliber looks so smooth and natural that it is easy to forget how many hours of hard work and perspiration are going on behind the scenes.

Now he was ready to start the 1999 PGA Tour with a completely overhauled game and a renewed sense of confidence. It was the new and improved Tiger!

16
Onward and Upward

After more than a solid year of studying with Coach Harmon, Tiger was ready to blossom into a fully mature player in 1999. But working on improving his golf skills was not the only form of practice Tiger had been doing. He had also been spending many hours working out and lifting weights, so that he would be stronger and more fit. Since he had gained at least twenty pounds of solid muscle, the strategy must have been a good one!

During his first two years on the PGA tour, the constant grind of travel and tournaments had been exhausting. Tiger was sure that the more physically fit he became, the easier it would be to withstand the rigors of being a professional athlete. In addition, he started running regularly to improve his aerobic endurance. Possibly the most difficult change of all was trying to eat a more healthy diet. If there was anything Tiger enjoyed, it was going to McDonald's! But he decided to make a conscious effort to keep fast food as an occasional treat, instead of a way of life.

In addition, Tiger tried to make a conscious effort to keep a certain amount of balance in his life. He wanted to be a great golfer, but that didn't mean that he had to give up all of the other activities he enjoyed, like going fishing and playing video games. He had stayed very close to a group of friends he had either grown up with or met at Stanford, and he made a point of hanging out with them regularly, even if that just meant sitting around and watching cartoons! Without taking the time to have fun and spend time with his family and friends, Tiger knew that playing golf might start to seem too much like *work*.

Tiger placed third in the first tournament of the year, the Mercedes Championships in January. Then he came in fifth in the Phoenix Open later that month. He was still adjusting to the mechanics of his new swing, but with every round he played, it felt better and better.

The next month, Tiger won his first tournament of 1999. It was the Buick Invitational, and he delivered a fantastic total score of twenty-two under par. He had always enjoyed playing in his home state of California, and it was especially exciting because his mother, Kultida, came to watch him. Tiger's father, Earl, had been having some health problems, so he was unable to travel as frequently as he had during the early days of Tiger's career. But he was certainly rooting for his son every step of the way!

At the Buick Invitational, Tiger set a course record in the third round with a staggeringly low score of 62. After that, there was no stopping him. The rest of the field kept trying to catch up, but Tiger had left them far behind. He finished off the tournament with a flashy, crowd-pleasing eagle on the 18th hole. It was fun to win, but it was even more fun to win with *style*.

In March, Tiger decided to make one final important change in his overall game. Although he had enjoyed his time working with his longtime caddy, Mike "Fluff" Cowan, both Tiger and Coach Harmon felt that it would be a good idea for Tiger to try switching to a new caddy. The relationship between a golfer and his or her caddy is a very delicate one, and it's important to find just the right fit. Even the smallest personality conflict could wreak havoc on a player's game. For someone as famous as Tiger, it was also crucial to find a caddy who would remain comfortable and relaxed, despite the relentless glare of the media and the huge crowds lining the fairways at every single tournament. Tiger was very protective of his privacy, and the ideal caddy for him would be a person who liked to keep a low profile and had no interest in giving interviews of any kind.

After some serious thought, Tiger selected Steve Williams to be his new caddy. Steve was a cheerful, laid-back guy, who was from New Zealand originally. He had been caddying for high-profile professional golfers for many years, so Tiger knew that Steve would have no trouble adjusting to the media circus that often surrounded him. Luckily, Tiger and Steve hit it off right away, and Tiger was especially pleased to discover that his new caddy knew when to joke around — and when it was time to be quiet and serious. Tiger was such an intense player, that sometimes he had to be reminded to enjoy himself! Steve was also an expert on golf, who knew exactly which club to pick, and which type of shot to try, in the wide variety of situations which can arise during any given tournament. All things considered, he gave every indication of being the perfect choice.

Tiger was still adapting to the newer aspects of his game, and so he struggled a little during the next few tournaments — including The Masters, where he ended up well out of contention in eighteenth place. He shot a personal career record low round of 61 at the Byron Nelson Classic, but was only tied for seventh place at the end of the tournament. But despite these setbacks, for the most part, his redesigned swing finally felt natural, and he was increasingly gaining confidence in it. Tiger was very disappointed not to have done better at The Masters, since the course in Augusta, Georgia, was one of his very favorite places to play. But he was still pleased with the progress he was making, even if the rest of the golfing world hadn't really noticed yet.

Then, in June, Tiger won the Memorial Tournament with a final score of fifteen strokes under par, and he placed third in the prestigious U.S. Open Championship. The U.S. Open is one of the four major tournaments, which include The Masters, the U.S. Open, the British Open, and the PGA Championship. Winning all four tournaments — a nearly impossible feat — is called the Grand Slam, and it is the ultimate goal of every ambitious golfer in the world. It has only been accomplished once, back in 1930, by a player named Bobby Jones. That year, Bobby won the U.S. Open, the British Open, the British Amateur, and the U.S. Amateur, which were the four big tournaments in those days. In the 1930s, it was considered much more respectable to play as an amateur than to be a professional golfer, so Bobby had retained his amateur status instead of joining the PGA Tour. But he still holds the record as the only single-season Grand Slam winner in golf history. Obviously, the Grand Slam is the record all professional golfers yearn to achieve, and the thought of winning a Grand Slam was one of Tiger's fondest dreams.

Following his third place finish in the U.S. Open, Tiger came up with another victory in the Motorola Western Open. Then, in August, he added a second career major to his resume when he took the PGA Championship. With his 1997 Masters victory, winning the PGA Championship brought him halfway to a career Grand Slam!

Only *four* other players had ever managed to do that, including the great Ben Hogan, Jack Nicklaus, Gary Player, and Gene Sarazen. Tiger hoped that he would be able to join that exalted group one day!

The PGA Championship had been a very exciting tournament. Tiger faced a strong challenge from a gifted nineteen-year-old rookie player from Spain named Sergio Garcia. Many golf observers hoped that this was the beginning of an exciting new rivalry, as the two players fought neck-and-neck throughout the competition.

Tiger was struggling to stay ahead of Sergio on the final day of the tournament, but his opponent just wouldn't go away. Whatever Tiger did, Sergio would promptly match. Then, on the back nine, disaster struck for Tiger! First, he hit a bogey on the 12th hole, and then he stunned a nation of viewers when he *double*-bogeyed the 13th. Was Tiger faltering under the pressure from the eager, young Sergio? It seemed as though he was on the verge of giving the tournament away.

But Tiger had learned how to slow down and sharpen his focus so intently that the rest of the world would just disappear. Instead of worrying about the bold challenger charging after him, Tiger knew it was time to concentrate exclusively on his *own* game. He promptly rallied back from the disaster at the 13th hole, and played solid, disciplined golf on each of the last five holes. Sergio stubbornly remained just one stroke behind, but

Tiger held on for the victory. He played the rest of the course perfectly, leaving himself with an uncomplicated putt on the 18th green. With one light swing, he dropped the ball neatly into the cup, and walked away with a win. He had risen to the occasion, and now he had another major championship on his record!

At the NEC-World Series of Golf championship tournament two weeks later, Tiger once again found himself challenged by Sergio Garcia. But in the third round, Tiger knocked Sergio — and all of the other players — completely out of contention by shooting a 62. He had missed shooting a 60 by a matter of inches, *literally* — but that is the way golf works. Sometimes a nearly impossible putt will roll into the cup, while an easier shot will just slither by. Golf is truly a game of inches.

In any case, Tiger's 62 was the second lowest score in course history, and he could hardly be disappointed by such a fine outing. On Sunday, none of the other players came close to making a serious threat to Tiger's lead, and he ended up with a ten under par score. Not only that, but he took home the largest prize of his career — an even million dollars!

Winning so much money for one tournament was thrilling, but Tiger was even more pleased by the results of the Ryder Cup. When he had been chosen to play for the team in 1997, neither he — nor the rest of his teammates — had done very well. The United States was defeated quite easily by the European team. This time, Tiger made a vow that things would be different!

The Ryder Cup is played every two years, and it alternates between courses in Europe and in the United States. In 1997, they had played in England, but in 1999, it was held in Massachusetts. The early part of the competition was close, and the European team steadily collected points towards a possible victory. In Ryder Cup competition, the first team to reach 14½ points, based upon the scores of the individual competitions, wins.

On the last day, the pressure was on Tiger and his teammates, who included stars like Justin Leonard, David Duval, Phil Mickelson, and Davis Love. The American team responded by winning six matches in a row, with Tiger contributing two victories personally. The United States won by a final score of 14½ to 13½. Winning was always fun, but Tiger was mainly pleased that he had represented his country so well, and been able to help his teammates regain the Ryder Cup. It was a nice change to be able to play solely for national pride.

At the end of the year, the Associated Press named Tiger the Male Athlete of the Year for 1999. Bicyclist Lance Armstrong, who had overcome cancer to win the Tour de France, came in second, and the brilliant Boston Red Sox pitcher Pedro Martinez received enough votes to take third place. It was the second time Tiger had won this award, and he was proud to be considered at all among such inspiring athletes. He also came away with his second ESPY Male Athlete of the Year prize, and took home the title of 1999 World Sportsman of the Year, too! These honors were richly deserved, since Tiger had finished off the season with eight PGA victories, a feat which hadn't been accomplished for a quarter of a century. He had also won three non-tour events, for a total of eleven victories. No other PGA player had managed to do *that* for fifty years. To top off a wonderful 1999, he became the first golfer in history to win over six million dollars in a single season.

It did not get much publicity at the time, but Tiger did something else that was very important that fall. After a great deal of consideration — and medical advice — Tiger decided to undergo sophisticated laser eye surgery, with the hope of markedly improving his vision. In recent years, more and more athletes — as well as members of the general public — have had this surgery done. It only works for certain types of vision problems, but Tiger was a good candidate for the procedure. Very few people knew that his eyes were actually quite weak, and despite the fact that the surgery had the potential to be a little bit risky, the thought of being able to see clearly was hard to resist. So Tiger agreed to have the laser operation, and it was very successful. Afterwards, his vision — without glasses or contact lenses — was tested to be 20-15. 20-20 is considered normal vision, and Tiger's vision was now significantly superior to that! If Tiger had been playing so brilliantly *without* perfect vision, how good would he be now? Tiger was delighted by the results of the operation, and hoped that it would have a positive impact on his playing.

All of the pieces were in place for Tiger to take his place at the top of the PGA, once and for all. Now he just had to wait for the new 2000 season to start!

17
A Brilliant Year

At the end of 1999, Tiger had won the last four PGA tournaments in a row, and he started off the new millennium by winning two more! First came the Mercedes Championships, where he beat Ernie Els on a two-hole play-off. Tiger was pushed to his limits, as both players came up with clutch eagles at the 18th hole to lead to the exciting finale. While they both birdied the first play-off hole, Ernie fell just short on the second hole, which meant that he could do no better than par the hole. Since Tiger hit another birdie, it didn't matter either way. Tiger had triumphed again!

That victory was his *fifth* consecutive win on the tour, which put him in a tie with Ben Hogan's well-known winning streak in 1953. But Tiger didn't stop there. Next came the National Pro-Am Tournament, which was held at the famous Pebble

Beach course. Pebble Beach may be the one place where all golfers, both professionals and amateurs, hope to play at least once in their lives. The course is located directly next to the Pacific Ocean, and the crashing waves on the shore below add a touch of drama and mystery to an already beautiful course. The unpredictable ocean winds also add a challenging dimension to mastering Pebble Beach!

On the last afternoon of the tournament, Tiger's chances of winning were very slim. He was behind by a full seven strokes — with only seven holes left to play! The leader was Matt Gogel, who was several years older than Tiger, but only playing his first year on the PGA Tour. While Matt made a valiant effort to hang on to what had seemed like an insurmountable lead, Tiger kept the pressure coming. He hit one great shot after another, including an astounding eagle shot on the 15th hole. By the final hole, Matt could only watch in horror as his overwhelming advantage evaporated for good. Tiger smacked one last birdie and won the tournament by shooting a 64.

Ben Hogan had also won six tournaments in a row in 1948, and now Tiger shared that accomplishment. Tiger assured reporters that it didn't really count, since his victories had taken place during two different years — but everyone else was still extremely impressed. The all-time record for consecutive tour victories is eleven, and was set by a player named Byron Nelson, back in 1945. Nelson had thoroughly trounced the competition during his amazing streak — and now Tiger was already more than halfway to matching him.

But, in the end, that record would have to wait for another time, because Tiger came in second at his next tournament, the Buick Invitational. He was trailing during the final round, but he made every effort to catch his opponent, Phil Mickelson. Phil hung on to win, though, and Tiger's streak was over. However, a different sort of record was set when the final round of play got higher ratings on television than the NBA All-Star game! Tiger may have lost, but the network airing the tournament definitely came out on top.

Tiger won two of the next six tournaments he played, and barely missed winning a third. He would have been equally competitive at The Masters, but he had an off-day during the first round and his score of 75 set him back too far to have any real chance of catching the eventual victor, veteran Vijay Singh. Tiger was disappointed, but knew that he would have other chances to regain the magic he had found at The Masters three years earlier.

The next major tournament scheduled was the U.S. Open. Tiger cruised easily to a record-setting fifteen stroke victory, completely crushing the rest of the players. That margin was even more impressive than his twelve stroke win in the 1997 Masters! This was the 100th time the U.S. Open tournament had been played, and Tiger had come up with the lowest score ever. In fact, fifteen strokes was the widest margin of victory for *any* of the major tournaments. The previous record of thirteen strokes had been set all the way back in 1862!

Tiger was happy about that, but since the final Sunday of the tournament took place on Father's Day, he thought his victory was an excellent tribute — and gift — to his still-ailing father, Earl. He knew his father would have spent the day glued to the television, and it felt good to be able to do something extra special for Earl to enjoy.

With the flood of new records mounting up, it began to seem as though Tiger's only *real* rivalry was with the very history of golf itself. Sometimes other players on the tour were able to challenge him — and even win tournaments here and there, but increasingly, he was competing against the Ghosts of Golf Past. Most golf experts would agree that Jack Nicklaus, Arnold Palmer, Bobby Jones, Ben Hogan, Sam Snead, and possibly Byron Nelson were the greatest players of all time. Tiger knew that he would never be satisfied until his name belonged in the same breath with the members of that elite group.

The next week, Tiger delighted the golfing world when he served as a caddy for his close friend Jerry Chang. Jerry was a terrific amateur golfer, and he was trying to qualify for the U.S. Amateur Public Links. Jerry missed the cut, but he still had a great day watching his famous pal lug *his* heavy golf bag around the course in the hot Nevada sunshine. The people attending the tournament were very surprised when they saw the best golfer in the world go ambling by as nothing more than a contented caddy.

After that, it was time for Tiger to start preparing for the next major tournament, the British Open. He spent some time in Ireland first, appearing at charity events and trying to relax by getting in some fishing. The British Open was going to be played at the St. Andrews course in Scotland, where golf had originally been invented. Tiger wanted to be as rested as possible for the challenge which lay ahead.

The first British Open was played in 1860, and St. Andrews had a well-deserved reputation for being a rugged course to play. Nestled among rocky crags, the course is notoriously windy, with very deep bunkers, and compact fairways and greens. Tiger was prepared to have a difficult time, but posted a 67 in the first round — and never looked back. By the time the tournament was over, he had set two more records with a nineteen under par final score, and a total of 269. The British Open had existed for one hundred and thirty years, and no one had ever played a better tournament there! Most impressively, in four days of play, Tiger did not hit a *single* ball into one of those treacherous bunkers.

The best part of all was that now Tiger had won a career Grand Slam, with at least one victory in each of the four majors! He was the fifth player in history to do this, following in the footsteps of the usual names Ben Hogan and Jack Nicklaus, and with the addition of Gary Player and Gene

Sarazen. If he had won The Masters earlier that year, he would have been only the second player since Bobby Jones to win the Grand Slam in a single season. Even so, he was now the second player to win *three* majors in one season, equaling Ben Hogan's mark set during his stellar 1953 season.

The PGA Championship was the final major of 2000, and obviously, Tiger was heavily favored to win. He was eager to play, because he was scheduled to be paired with a very special partner. The great Jack Nicklaus, known as The Golden Bear, was sixty years old, and this was the last time he was planning to play at the PGA Championship. Tiger had never played with his childhood hero before in a professional tournament, and he couldn't help being awed by the prospect.

It ended up being a very memorable occasion. To no one's surprise, he started off with a bang by delivering a 66 in the first round. And for once, Tiger was not the center of attention while he was playing, and he enjoyed the novelty of feeling — almost — anonymous, as the thousands of spectators paid homage to one of the greatest players of all time playing his final round at this major. Jack did not score high enough to make the cut, but he and Tiger still had a great time making their way around the course. They each finished the second round with a flourish, by hitting twin birdies on the 18th hole. Jack might be leaving the tour, but he would never be forgotten — especially by Tiger.

"I enjoyed playing with Jack and it was great for me," Tiger told the press afterwards, as reported by Clifton Brown of the *New York Times*. "Nobody even noticed what I was doing. . . . It was an honor to play with Jack. To be honest, though, when I am on that first tee, I could care less who I am playing with. I am trying to put myself in position to win a major championship."

At his own press conference, Jack was very enthusiastic about what he had observed while playing with Tiger. "He shot the easiest 66 today, and he missed half a dozen opportunities," Jack Nicklaus told the gathered reporters, as quoted by George Willis of the *New York Post*. "Phenomenal control, phenomenal concentration. Most of his shots were so well within himself that 66 was just a piece of cake. That was a real treat to watch."

Although most of the attention was being given to Jack and Tiger, other players were surging forward with strong rounds of their own. By the time the third round began, Scott Dunlap was sharing the lead with Tiger. It had rained the night before, which made the fairways softer and more forgiving than they would ordinarily be. That set the stage for many players to shoot lower scores than usual. Jose Olazabal, in particular, set a blazing pace with a round of 63, and while Scott Dunlap began to lose some ground, a rather obscure player named Bob May began making his own bid for the lead.

During all of this, surprisingly, Tiger was floundering. On a day when other people were playing so well, he struggled all afternoon. He still managed to finish the day with a below-par 70, but it had been hard, grinding work with every single shot. He was still in the lead, but half a dozen other players were now in a legitimate position to win the next day.

For the final round, Tiger was paired with Bob May. Bob had grown up in the same area of Southern California, and he had been a successful junior player when Tiger was still just learning how to play. He had always admired Bob, who was seven years older, and had hoped that he would someday be as successful on the junior circuit. As we now know, Tiger more than lived up to *that* particular goal.

Bob had had trouble qualifying for the PGA tour over the years, so he had spent most of his career playing in Europe. This was his first time ever at the PGA Championship, and here he was with a chance to defeat his boyhood friend, Tiger Woods!

As the afternoon passed, all of the other players dropped back with bogeys, double bogeys, and other mistakes. But Tiger and Bob were able to measure up to each other with each hole. As the day wore on, they played better and better, both of them shooting a 31 over the final nine holes.

The two were tied right up until the 18th hole, when they each hit the green with a chance to putt for the win. The 18th green had an unusual hilly design, and Tiger's ball had landed in an awkward uphill position. Bob's ball was further away from the pin, but was sitting in a position suited for a possible birdie putt. Bob made his shot, and the pressure was on. If Tiger missed, Bob would win the championship.

Tiger took his time examining the slope of the hill, using all of his concentration to focus on the path his ball would need to take. It was a very challenging shot, which would require impeccable timing and a light touch.

Tiger needed perfection — and that's what he delivered! He struck the ball gently, and everyone in the huge crowd seemed to stop breathing at once as they watched the ball start its slow curve towards the hole. Would it go in? *Could* it go in? Yes! Tiger had made the shot, and he and Bob had finished the tournament in a dead-heat.

Now it was time for a three-hole play-off. The player with the lowest score would go home with the fabled Wanamaker Trophy, which is given to the winner of the PGA Championship each year.

The play-off was set to start at the 16th hole, and Tiger and Bob would have to work their way back to the 18th hole. Tiger looked extremely calm, although he must have been nervous. He birdied the 16th without much trouble, while Bob only managed to shoot par. That gave Tiger a one stroke lead with two holes to play.

To the amazement of everyone watching, on the second play-off hole, Tiger drove his ball right off the course! It flew over the rough, hit a tree, and rolled down a path. Bob had a tremendous opportunity to even the score, since Tiger had little hope of recovering from such an awkward lie. But Bob

111

must have succumbed to a split second of nervousness, because his own shot went wide to the right and into the rough.

Somehow, Tiger had to find a way to aim his ball through trees and back up onto the course. With almost no hesitation, he smacked a hard, low drive and miraculously brought his ball back into play. After that, Tiger and Bob each held par, and now there was only one hole left. If Bob could not pick up a stroke from Tiger, the tournament was over. If he *did* make up a stroke, they would begin another play-off round.

Bob had not been able to capitalize on the golden opportunity he had been given on the second hole, but he got one more chance when Tiger's third hole ball ended up in a bunker well below the 18th green. But Tiger calmly flipped the ball right out of the bunker, and it landed close enough to the hole to make a par shot a near-certainty.

Bob was on the green, but he would have to produce a very long birdie shot to stop Tiger. At first, it looked as though he was going to succeed, but his ball spun just past the hole and rolled off to the side. Tiger bounded up to the green, and nudged his ball into the cup with a satisfying thump. The match was over, and Tiger had won his second consecutive PGA Championship!

"It's got to go down as one of the best duels in the game," Tiger said later, as was reported by sportswriter Hank Gola of the *New York Daily News*. "It was one memorable battle and I enjoyed it. We never backed off from one another . . .

birdie for birdie, shot for shot. That's as good as it gets."

It had been an incredible match — and with four months left in the season, Tiger had already put together what may end up being the most remarkable year in golfing history!

18
A True Master

Any normal human being might have had a small letdown after the spellbinding heroics of the PGA Championship, but Tiger came right back and won his next two tournaments, giving him a total of *nine* PGA victories by the end of September. With several events left to play in 2000, he was on his way to breaking yet another seemingly untouchable PGA record.

At the NEC Invitational Media Day press conference, Tiger told the media that despite his extraordinary year, he was still struggling to correct certain aspects of his game. "It takes time, a lot of hard work and patience," he explained. "It's starting to come around where the moves I'm making, I can just do it naturally without having to think about it. . . . Those things don't happen very often, where you feel calm about yourself, your emotions, your game. . . . When you finally hit one right, exactly the way you want to, feel just absolutely everything you want to feel on the golf swing come together, *that's* why we play."

Tiger may have sounded as though he still felt as though his game could use some improvements, but that didn't stop him from winning the tournament with an impressive twenty-one under par final score. This included shooting a 61 in the second round, which almost certainly destroyed the morale of the rest of the players — even though very few of them would have admitted it aloud.

The next tournament was the Bell Canadian Open. Interestingly, this was the same tournament for which Tiger hadn't even made the *cut* during his first year on the tour. But the eager twenty-one-year-old rookie from 1997 was an entirely different player from the dominant, seasoned golfer of 2000. This time, Tiger not only made the cut, but he also took home first place and a few new records!

Yet another relatively unknown player had come close to winning the tournament, and this time, it was Grant Waite, from New Zealand. On the very last hole of the final round, Grant had an excellent chance to win an upset victory when Tiger's ball went sailing into a deep bunker behind a water hazard. Grant knew that it would be almost impossible for Tiger to recover from that position without losing a stroke or two. If Tiger attempted to drive his ball out of the bunker across the water, instead of making a more conservative shot, he ran the risk of losing everything. Grant was *sure* that not even Tiger would have the nerve to try and drive the ball all the way across the water to try and hit the tiny strip of green behind it, without rolling back into the pond.

Except that, naturally, Tiger did just that! Fearlessly, he drove the ball right over the water, and it landed gently behind the 18th hole. Grant — along with throngs of spectators and people watching at home — was utterly stunned. *No one* should have been capable of making that shot with so little room for error. But, once again, the golfing world was reminded that Tiger was a genuine phenomenon. Grant could only watch as Tiger flicked his putt into the hole for a birdie, and won the tournament by a single stroke. His total score of 266 for four rounds was the lowest score produced during the entire twenty-two-year history of the Canadian Open.

That record was impressive enough by itself, but Tiger had accomplished something far more prestigious. By winning the U.S. Open, the British Open, and the PGA Championship in the same year, he became only the second player in history to win what is known as the Triple Crown. Lee Trevino had managed to do it back in 1971, but no one else had come close to matching him in almost thirty years. Now Tiger not only had a career Grand Slam, but he also had a Triple Crown!

There are quite a few records left for Tiger to tackle, most notably Jack Nicklaus's towering achievement of eighteen career victories in the four major tournaments. This record has always been considered one which could never be broken by anyone — but the same is true for many of the records Tiger has *already* demolished.

At only twenty-four, Tiger is still extremely young for a professional golfer. He could easily play professionally for another twenty or thirty years! Even Tiger himself probably can't quite imagine how many records he may be capable of setting during his career. But it is a safe bet that he will continue to try every single time he steps onto a golf course.

As the years pass, can Tiger keep improving as a player? Is such a thing even possible? How good can he become? How many records will he break? Is he the best golfer who has ever been born? It will take years to find out the answers to these questions, but golf fans everywhere will enjoy watching Tiger on his continuing journey to greatness.

Tiger's goal is to be the best golfer who ever lived, and he is certainly already well on his way!

But one of the most exciting things about sports is knowing that someday, somewhere, another young player — it might be a boy; it might be a girl — will come along to try and surpass Tiger's achievements. Right now, this player may already be competing on the junior level, or he or she might just be beginning to learn how to play, without even realizing that greatness lies ahead.

This unknown player might even be you!

Golf: A Brief History

The game of golf has been around for centuries, but no one is really sure when, where, or even *how* it began. The general theory is that, starting in medieval times, people would sometimes use sticks to hit small rocks around pastures or meadows. To make the game more interesting, they began trying to hit targets, and knock the pebbles into holes in the ground. Over the years, this gradually developed into the game we now call golf.

The word *golfe* was first mentioned in Scotland in the 1300s. In 1457, King James II actually banned the game! The king felt that people were spending so much time playing golf, they were neglecting to practice their archery. Since archery was considered a major aspect of the country's military defense, King James II took this very seriously, and so he outlawed the game.

But, despite the law against golf, people in Scotland kept playing. The geography in Scotland was naturally suited to golf, because there was lots of flat ground and plenty of sandy areas near the ocean. This natural terrain was used as the earliest kind of golf course. Golf courses were not intentionally built or designed for many years.

In 1744, a Scottish golf club called the Honourable Company of Edinburgh Golfers was established. Ten years later, in 1754, the most famous golf club in the world, The Royal and Ancient Golf Club of St. Andrews, opened. Official rules were developed, and the game of golf became more formal. Soon, there were courses and tournaments all over Scotland, and the game gradually spread over to England and Ireland, too. In 1860, the first British Open was played. Even today, this is considered one of the most important tournaments in the world.

When Scottish immigrants came to the United States, they brought the game of golf with them. In 1888, the first American club was founded by a recent immigrant named John Reid. The club was named after Scotland's St. Andrews golf club, and it was located in Yonkers, New York. After that, golf clubs and courses began to spring up all over the country.

In 1894, the United States Golf Association was formed. The U.S.GA is still the major governing body for American golf today. The first U.S. Open Tournament was played the following year. Then, in 1916, the Professional Golfers' Association, or

PGA, was instituted, and the PGA Tour began. The Ladies Professional Golf Association, or LPGA, came along in 1950. Finally, in 1980, the Senior PGA Tour was created. This way, players who had retired from the PGA could continue to compete professionally.

Traditionally, golf has always been considered an elite, exclusive, and expensive sport. As a rule, only the wealthiest members of society could afford to join country clubs, and learn how to play golf. For many years, most clubs would only admit male Caucasian members. People who wanted to join were often excluded on the basis of religion, race, and gender. Today, most of these ugly traditions have faded away, and we can only hope that one day, they will be a distant memory. Also, in addition to private clubs, most cities and towns now have public golf courses and driving ranges available. That way, everyone can participate.

The first really famous American player was Bobby Jones. In 1930, Bobby won all four of the major golf tournaments of the time: the U.S. Open, the British Open, the British Amateur Championship, and the U.S. Amateur Championship. Bobby was a well-known public figure, and helped make the game more popular in this country.

Other famous American players over the years have included Ben Hogan, Jack Nicklaus, Sam Snead, Arnold Palmer, and Babe Didrikson Zaharias. President Dwight Eisenhower loved the game of golf, and during his presidency, many Americans began to play for the first time. Other presidents like Gerald Ford, George Bush, and Bill Clinton have also been enthusiastic about the game.

In the modern era, players like Lee Trevino, Nancy Lopez, Tom Watson, Greg Norman, and Nick Faldo have gathered headlines. After less than five years as a professional golfer, it seems clear that Tiger Woods is destined to join this list of all-time great players. In fact, Tiger may end up being the most famous and successful golfer ever!

Golf Etiquette

Golf is a very civilized sport, and there are a number of informal traditions that players observe. In golf, courtesy and respect are considered as important as actually playing the game. There are a number of unwritten basic etiquette rules, and golfers are expected to obey all of them.

1. When another player is getting ready to hit the ball, no one else should talk, move around, or interfere in any way. A player should never disturb anyone else's concentration, or stand in his or her line of vision.

2. Whether you are playing in teams, or in pairs, the player with the lowest score on the previous hole gets to tee off first on the next hole. This is known as having "the honor."

3. A player should wait until everyone is out of the way before hitting his or her ball. If a ball is likely to hit someone else, you are expected to shout the word *fore* as a warning. If someone shouts "Fore!" at *you*, be sure to duck!

4. Players should not delay the game for any unnecessary reasons. When it is your turn to take a shot, don't waste time.

5. If a player is searching for a lost ball, he or she must allow other players to "play through," and continue with their games. The player must then wait for everyone else to go by, before he or she can resume playing.

6. After driving a ball out of a bunker (or sand trap), a player must fill any holes he or she made. Most of the time, players will even rake the sand smooth for the next player who might come along.

7. If a player raises a divot, or in any way damages the grass, he or she must stop and fix the spot right away by gently pushing the turf back in place. This is particularly important if a player makes any ball or spike marks on the putting green.

8. All flagsticks must be replaced in the cup before a player can move on to the next hole. Also, players must be very careful not to damage the putting green by dropping the flagstick, putting their golf bags onto the delicate ground, or leaning on their clubs.

9. As soon as a player has finished playing the hole, he or she must leave the putting green right away.

10. It is considered improper to run on a golf course, especially on the putting green.

11. When on the course, a player should always be sure to hit the right ball! It is a good idea to mark your golf balls in some way so that you won't make a mistake.

12. Always practice good sportsmanship, and shake hands with your opponent when the round is over.

Golf: The Basics

In the simplest terms, golf is a game in which you try to hit a small white ball into a series of holes in the ground. People who love golf *really love* golf. To the outsider, the game may sometimes seem a little bit dull or frustrating, but fans feel that golf is one of the most challenging and exciting sports in the world.

A golf course consists of eighteen holes. Each hole is made up of three parts: the tee box, the fairway, and the putting green. On every golf course, there are both natural and intentional obstacles. Natural obstacles include trees, hills, and the wind. Intentional obstacles are the bunkers, water hazards, and "rough" areas placed in strategic locations on each course. Golfers enjoy the challenge of trying to avoid these pitfalls.

Players start a round of golf in the tee box area,

which is sometimes called the tee box. The goal of the game is to hit the ball down along each of the eighteen fairways to the putting greens, and then, into each hole. At all times, the player tries to hit the ball into the hole with as few strokes as possible.

Each course has established an ideal number of strokes to complete the eighteen holes, and this number is known as par for that course. Generally, par is somewhere between 70 and 72. Individual holes are also graded by a par standard. They are usually par-3, par-4, or par-5 holes. Every now and then, a course has a par-6 hole, but this is rare. Basically, this all means that an expert player would need that many shots to complete that particular hole. For example, if a player needs four shots to finish a par-3 hole, then he or she has gone over par. If a player needs only four shots to finish a par-5 hole, then he or she is under par. The goal of the game is to stay under par, whenever possible.

There are two different forms of scoring. One method is based on the number of total strokes a player needs to complete the course. This is called medal, or stroke, play, and the player with the lowest number wins. In match play, the player who wins the most individual *holes* wins the game. Most professional tournaments use medal play. Players are judged on the number of total strokes they take, over a period of several days and through several rounds.

To play well, a golfer needs to use the right

equipment. The earliest golf balls were made out of wood. These balls broke easily, so companies began making leather balls that were stuffed with feathers. Obviously, these balls could not travel very far and easily got waterlogged. In later years, balls were made out of rubber. Today, golf balls usually consist of a compressed rubber core, covered with some type of hard plastic.

The first golf clubs were made out of wood, and hickory was the most popular choice. However, these clubs were hard to control and not very durable. In 1929, a rule was passed by the U.S.GA allowing players to use metal clubs. Often, the club head was still made out of wood, but the long shaft was steel. In addition to steel, today's players use clubs made out of fiberglass, aluminum, titanium, and countless other new composites.

A player is allowed to carry a maximum of fourteen clubs during any round of golf. There are several different types, although all clubs consist of a grip, a shaft, and a club head. The group of clubs known as woods are used to hit the ball long distances. The woods are usually numbered from one to five. The 1-wood, the most powerful club in a player's arsenal, is referred to as the driver, and many players use this club to tee off. It is the longest and strongest club, and so it will hit the ball farther than any other club in the golf bag.

Another group of clubs a player can use are called irons. The irons are more delicate, and are used for shorter shots, which require more control and accuracy. These clubs are generally numbered from one to nine. The 9-iron is the shortest and most angular of the irons, and it is able to lift the ball for high, short shots. When a player uses irons with lower numbers, the ball will travel somewhat farther and not quite as high.

Finally, most players will carry a sand wedge, a pitching wedge, and a putter. The wedges are mainly used to loft balls up and out of sand traps. The club heads on the wedges are angled sharply backward, so it is easy to get underneath the ball. There are many different kinds of putters, but the club heads almost always have flat fronts. When the flat side strikes the ball, the golfer is able to maintain lots of control and precision. This is desperately needed on the putting green.

Hundreds of different brands of golf clubs are manufactured today, and every player will make individual choices. The average club player will carry a driver (or 1-wood), a 3-wood, a 5-wood, irons 3 through 9, a sand wedge, a pitching wedge, and a putter. Some players like very long clubs; some do not. Others like very flexible clubs, while some prefer stiff clubs. In any case, only long hours of practice will help a player decide exactly which clubs he or she wants to use. The strategic aspects of knowing which club to select for a particular shot can take *years* to master.

Finally, a player must wear proper golf shoes on the course, so that the turf will not be damaged. These special shoes are usually made of leather and have some sort of spiked soles. Many players also like to wear gloves, and some also choose hats and sunglasses. Lots of golf courses have dress codes, and a certain fashion protocol is generally followed. On the whole, players are supposed to look neat and conservative. Jeans, sneakers, and T-shirts are usually not permitted. Some clubs don't even allow players to wear shorts! Bright colors tend to be very popular, and some players look downright gaudy in their outfits. However, once you accept the fact that these traditions are part of the golf experience, they can make the game seem even more fun.

An eighteen-hole golf course is usually six or seven thousand feet long. Because of this, players who walk get plenty of exercise. Some players like to carry their own golf bags, while others hire caddies to do it for them. Some golf bags have wheels attached and can be pulled around the course. There are also players who prefer to ride around the course in small golf carts, but only on the Senior PGA tour are professionals allowed to do this.

Golf is a game that requires a lot of special equipment and appropriate facilities, so it is difficult to play the game casually. Buying a set of clubs is a serious investment, and a player would want to make sure that these clubs would get plenty of use in order to justify the expense. Fortunately, both public and private areas offer both lessons and equipment rentals. That way, it is easy for people to find out if they enjoy the game without spending much money. The best thing about golf is that it can be played at any age, and it doesn't require any unusual physical abilities. It is a game that anyone can learn, and once you start, most people play for the rest of their lives.

Golf has never been as popular as sports like football, basketball, and baseball are in this country. However, as more and more people are exposed to the game, that is starting to change. For all we know, twenty years from now, golf may be the biggest sport in the country! In any case, golf has been around for many centuries, and it is a sport that anyone can enjoy.

Career Highlights

Childhood (Ages 2–13)

When Tiger was only two years old, he was a guest on *The Mike Douglas Show* along with celebrities Bob Hope and Jimmy Stewart. In a live exhibition on national television, Tiger outputted Bob Hope, a well-known amateur golfer. This clip was also shown on the *CBS Network News*.

At the age of three, Tiger scored a remarkable 48 strokes, while playing a full nine holes on a U.S. Navy golf course.

That same year, Tiger won a pitch, putt, and drive competition, defeating opponents who were ten and eleven years old!

As a five-year-old, Tiger appeared on the network television show *That's Incredible*. In the next few years, he was also featured on *The Today Show*, and *Good Morning, America*. Before he was thirteen, Tiger had been on all of the major networks, as well as ESPN.

Tiger won the Optimist International Junior Championship four times (at the ages of eight, nine, twelve, and thirteen).

At thirteen, he came in second in the Insurance Youth Golf Classic National Tournament.

Junior and Amateur Career

General Achievements

Three-time U.S. Amateur Champion, and the only player ever to accomplish this feat (three consecutive victories)

Selected four times as a First Team, Rolex Junior, All-American (1990–1993)

Selected four times to play in the Canon Cup, representing the West team, 1990–1993

Selected twice as the Rolex Junior Player of the Year

Second, all-time, on the AJGA Career Wins List, with eight AJGA Championships

The only three-time winner of the U.S. Junior Amateur Championship (consecutive victories)

Won a total of six World Junior Amateur titles

Youngest player ever to win the U.S. Amateur Championship

Only player of African-American ancestry ever to win the U.S. Amateur Championship

Youngest player ever to win a U.S. Junior Amateur Championship

Youngest player ever to win the Insurance Youth Golf Classic National

Youngest player ever to participate in a PGA tournament

Named Southern California Player of the Year four years in a row

Played in the Southern California/French Junior Cup in Paris, France

Named in 1995 by *GQ* magazine as one of the "Top 50 Most Influential People in the Next 10 Years"

A two-time selection to the First Team, All-American

A two-time AJGA Player of the Year

A six-time winner of the Optimist International Golf Junior Championship

High School

Age 14

Winner, Optimist International Golf Junior Championship

Winner, Insurance Youth Golf Classic National (Independent Insurance Agent Junior Classic)

Youngest winner in history of Insurance Youth Golf Classic National

Came in second, PGA National Junior Championship

Placed third, U.S. Junior Amateur Championship

Selected as the Southern California Player of the Year

Selected to play in the Southern California/French Junior Cup in Paris, France

Age 15

Winner, U.S. Junior Amateur Championship

Youngest player ever to win the U.S. Junior Amateur Championship

Winner, Optimist International Golf Junior Championship

Winner, Southern California Junior Championship

Winner, AJGA Ping/Phoenix Junior Championship

Winner, AJGA Lake Tahoe Junior Classic

Winner, Los Angeles City Junior Championship

Winner, Orange Bowl Junior International Tournament

Winner, CIF-SCGA High School Invitational Championship (individual, not team)

Selected as the AJGA Player of the Year

Selected as the *Golf Digest* Player of the Year

Selected as the Southern California Player of the Year

Selected as the Titleist-*Golfweek* National Amateur of the Year

Chosen to the First Team, Rolex Junior, All-American

Age 16

Winner, U.S. Junior Amateur Championship

Winner, AJGA Ping/Phoenix Junior Championship

Winner, AJGA Nabisco Mission Hills Desert Junior Championship

Winner, AJGA ProGear San Antonio Shoot-Out

Came in second, Optimist International Golf Junior Championship

Ranked in the top thirty-two players, 1992 U.S. Amateur

Selected as the AJGA Player of the Year

Selected as the *Golf Digest* Player of the Year

Selected as the Southern California Player of the Year

Selected as the Titleist-*Golfweek* National Amateur of the Year

Named the *Golf World* Player of the Year

Played in his first two professional tournaments as an amateur: the PGA Los Angeles Open and the U.S. Open Sectional Qualifying

Age 17

Winner, U.S. Junior Amateur Championship

Winner, Southern California Junior Best Ball Championship

Ranked in the top thirty-two players, 1993 U.S. Amateur

Selected to the First Team, Rolex Junior, All-American

Played in three PGA tournaments: the Los Angeles Open, the Honda Classic, and the Byron Nelson Classic, as well as the U.S. Open Sectional Qualifying

Named the *Golf World* Player of the Year

Selected as the Southern California Player of the Year

Winner of the Dial Award for 1993, given to the top high school athlete in the country

Agreed to accept a full scholarship to prestigious Stanford University

Age 18

Winner, U.S. Amateur Championship

Youngest player ever to win the U.S. Amateur Championship

Winner, Western Amateur Championship

Winner, Pacific Northwest Amateur Championship

Winner, Southern California Golf Association Amateur Championship

Winner, CIF Southern Section Championship

Semifinalist, California State Amateur Championship

Played in three PGA tournaments: the Nestlé Invite, the Buick Classic, and the Motorola Western Open

Also played in the Johnny Walker Asian Classic in Thailand

Named *Los Angeles Times* Player of the Year

Chosen as the Orange County Player of the Year

Selected as the Orange County League MVP

College Career

Freshman Year

Entered Stanford University as a freshman, fall 1994

Named *Golf World*'s Man of the Year

Winner of his first collegiate tournament, the William Tucker Invitational

Member, U.S. Team at the World Amateur Championships, played in France. With Tiger's help, the United States won.

Nominated for the coveted Sullivan Award, given each year to the best amateur athlete in the country

Played in his first major professional tournament, The Masters; he was the only amateur to qualify for the tournament, and won a silver medal for finishing low amateur

Tied for fifth place, NCAA Championships

Played in the British Open

Played for the United States team in the Walker Cup

Chosen the 1995 Pac-10 Player of the Year

Named Stanford's 1995 Male Freshman of the Year

Selected as a Pre-Season First Team, All-American by *Golfweek* magazine

Named to the First Team, All-American (after 1995 season)

Sophomore Year

1996 NCAA Champion

Winner of the Jack Nicklaus Award for the top male collegiate Golfer of the Year

Given the Arete Award for Courage in Sports

Received the Fred Haskins Award, for the most outstanding collegiate golfer

Co-winner of the Al Master Award, given to the outstanding athlete at Stanford University

Selected to the First Team, All-American

Chosen the Pac-10 Golfer of the Year

Selected to the First Team, All-Pacific-10 Conference

Set a course record by shooting a 61 in the Pac-10 Championship

Set a new Pac-10 record by scoring a tournament-low 270 strokes in the Pac-10 Championships

Set a course record by shooting a 67 in the NCAA
    Championships
Named the Rolex College Player of the Year
Winner, NCAA West Regional Championship
Winner, Pacific-10 Championship
Set a new all-time Pac-10 Championship record
    by scoring a 270 over the four-day tourna-
    ment
Set a course record in the Pac-10 championships
    with an all-time low score of 61 for an individ-
    ual round of golf

Professional Career Achievements

1997 Masters Champion
Won his first professional major tournament in
    his very first try, by an unprecedented 12 strokes
Was the fastest PGA player to go over $1,000,000
    in professional earnings, accomplishing this
    feat in only nine tournaments
Winner of the 1997 Asian Honda Classic
Won the first PGA Tournament of 1997, the Mer-
    cedes Championships
Winner, 1996 Disney World/Oldsmobile Golf Clas-
    sic
Winner, 1996 Las Vegas Invitational (his first pro-
    fessional win)
Set a course record by shooting a remarkable 59
    in a practice round at Isleworth, in Florida
Set a tournament record in The Masters by hitting
    an all-time low eighteen strokes under par,

breaking a thirty-year-old record of seventeen under par set by Jack Nicklaus in 1965

Made history with a twelve-stroke margin of victory in The Masters; the only player ever to post a wider margin of victory in a major championship was Tom Morris, in 1862

Was the youngest player to win *any* major Grand Slam event since Gene Sarazen in 1922

Out of 360 total Grand Slam events ever played, only one other golfer has ever equaled Tiger's total of eighteen under par (Nick Faldo, in the 1990 British Open)

Was the youngest player ever to win the Masters

Was the first minority (African-American or Asian-American) to win one of professional golf's four major tournaments

Is the first professional player in fourteen years to post five consecutive top-five finishes in PGA events

Selected as the 1996 *Sports Illustrated* Sportsman of the Year; one of only five golfers ever to be given this honor

Given ESPN's ESPY Award for being the Breakthrough Athlete of the Year

Named the 1996 PGA Tour Rookie of the Year

ESPY Male Athlete of the Year in 1997, and 1999

Chosen as the 1999 World Sportsman of the Year

Was the 1997 and 1999 Player of the Year, as selected by both the PGA of America, and the Golf Writers Association of America

Voted the 1997 and 1999 winner of the Jack Nicklaus Player of the Year Award, by the PGA Tour

Associated Press Male Athlete of the Year in 1997 and 1999

Winner of the Byron Nelson Award

Winner of the Vardon Trophy in 1999, given to the player who finishes with the lowest season-long scoring average. Tiger's average score-per-round of 68.43 was also the lowest in the history of professional golf

Winner of the 2000 Palm Performance Award for the player who performs the best in the West Coast PGA Tour events

A member of the winning United States Ryder Cup team in 1999; also played for the United States in 1997

Winner of the McCormack Award in 1998 and 1999, presented to the player who ranks first on the PGA Tour for the most weeks (43 in 1998, 37 in 1999)

Reached a number one ranking on the professional tour faster than any other player in history (after only 42 weeks on the PGA Tour), and was also the youngest golfer ever to do so

The first player to win three majors (the four major Tournaments are The Masters, the U.S. Open, the British Open, and the PGA Championship) in a single year since Ben Hogan won three in 1953

Was declared the Majors Aggregate Champion in 1999, for having the lowest total score in all four majors played that year

In 1999, he was the first player to win at least eight PGA events in one year since 1974

In 2000, Tiger became the first player to win at least *nine* PGA Tournaments in one season since 1950, setting this record by the end of the summer

In 2000, signed the highest endorsement deal (from Nike) offered to any athlete in history

The first player to win the PGA Championship two years in a row since 1937

Has already achieved a career Grand Slam, by winning each of the four major tournaments at least once, and is the youngest player ever to accomplish this feat. Only four other players have *ever* won a career Grand Slam

Has the record for the lowest total score in *each* of the majors. (He is tied with Bob May for a record of 18 under par in the PGA Championship, but is in sole possession of the record for each of the other three Majors)

Tiger leads all active (non-retired) PGA players in the number of career victories he has won

Named Golfer of the Decade (1990s) at the ESPN ESPY Awards

On track to become the first athlete in any sport ever to earn one *billion* dollars, including endorsements

A Look at the Numbers

Tiger's National Junior Tournament Record

1990 Season

Tournament Name	Place	Scores
Independent Insurance Agent Junior Classic (Insurance Youth Golf Classic)	1st	70–73–69–74 — 286
PGA Junior Classic	2nd	73–74–69–72 — 288
U.S. Junior Amateur	3rd (tie)	(match play)

Match play is a different form of scoring. Instead of counting the total number of strokes, the golfer who wins the most *holes* wins the match. See glossary for more information.

1991 Season

Tournament Name	Place	Scores
AJGA Taylor Made Woodlands Junior Classic	3rd	72–71 — 143
AJGA Ping/Phoenix Junior Championship	1st	72–70 — 142
AJGA USF&G Junior Classic	5th	79–74–70–72 — 295
AJGA Nabisco Mission Hills Desert Junior	1st	72–71–73 — 216
AJGA Las Vegas Founders' Legacy Junior	4th	70–76–69 — 215
AJGA Lake Tahoe	1st	73–71 — 144

Classic (Edgewood)

Optimist International Golf Junior Championship	1st	74–70–73–69 — 286
U.S. Junior Amateur	1st	(match play)
Independent Insurance Agent Junior Classic (Insurance Youth Golf Classic)	5th	unavailable

1992 Season

Tournament Name	Place	Scores
1991 AJGA Rolex Junior Classic	1st	77–79 (match play)
1991 Orange Bowl International Junior	1st	69–67–70–66 — 272
AJGA Taylor Made Woodlands Junior Classic	2nd (tie)	37–34 — 71
AJGA Ping/Phoenix Junior Championship	1st	69–69 — 138
AJGA Nabisco Mission Hills Desert Junior	1st	72–70–74 — 216
AJGA ProGear San Antonio Shoot-Out	1st	68–72–70 — 210
Western Junior Championship	5th (tie)	72–74 (match play)
AJGA Rolex Tournament of Champions	20th (tie)	77–75–69–77 — 298
Optimist International Golf Junior	2nd	68–71–68–75 — 282

Championship

U.S. Junior Amateur	1st	68–75 (match play)
AJGA Boys Junior Championship	1st	65–73–68–68 — 274
Independent Insurance Agent Junior Classic (Insurance Youth Golf Classic)	1st	68–70–69–73 — 280

1993 Season

Tournament Name	Place	Scores
1992 AJGA Rolex Junior Classic	9th (tie)	78–72 (match play)
1992 Orange Bowl International Junior	2nd (tie)	72–68–71–74 — 285
AJGA Taylor Made Woodlands Junior Classic	2nd (tie)	73–73 — 146
Optimist International Golf Junior Championship	4th	70–71–70–75 — 286
U.S. Junior Amateur	1st	69–74 (match play)
AJGA Lake Tahoe Classic	8th (tie)	73–76 — 149

1994–1995 Tournament Results

Tournament Name	Place	Scores
William Tucker Invitational	1st	68–72–68 — 208

Ping/*Golfweek* Preview	4th (tie)	72–72 — 141
Jerry Pate Invitational	1st	71–68–67 — 206
Golf World/Palmetto Dunes Collegiate	13th (tie)	70–66–80 — 216
Taylor Made/Big Island Intercollegiate	2nd	67–69–71 — 207
John A. Burns Intercollegiate	9th (tie)	75–68 — 143
Oregon Duck Invitational	4th	70–75 — 145
Southwestern Intercollegiate	2nd (tie)	75–72–72 — 219
Carpet Capital Classic	2nd	75–69–72 — 219
Thunderbird/ASU Intercollegiate	12th (tie)	71–70–79 — 220
U.S. Intercollegiates	WD (withdrew due to injury)	73–WD–WD
NCAA West Regionals	18th (tie)	72–72–72 — 216
NCAA Championships	5th (tie)	73–72–70–71 — 286

1995–1996 Tournament Results

Tournament Name	Place	Scores
Windon Memorial Classic	2nd	72–75–67 — 214
USF Invitational	6th (tie)	72–74–74 — 220

Stanford Invitational	1st	69–69–68 — 206
Golf World Collegiate	2nd	70–70–70 — 210
Ping Intercollegiate Raven Golf Club	2nd	68–69–69 — 206
John A. Burns Invitational	1st	73–71–69 — 213
Golf Digest Collegiate	23rd (tie)	70–77–77 — 224
Cleveland Golf Championships	1st	72–69–72 — 213
U.S. Collegiate	3rd	73–68–71 — 212
Tri-Match (Stanford, ASU, Arizona)	1st	69–71 — 140
Cougar Classic	1st	69–73–75 — 217
Pac-10 Championship	1st	61–65–73–71 — 270
NCAA West Regional	1st	68–70–67 — 205
NCAA Championships	1st	69–67–69–80 — 285

Tiger's Professional Statistics

1996 PGA Results

Tournament Name	Place	Scores
The Masters (amateur status)	Cut	75–75 — 150 (+6)(over par)

U.S. Open (amateur status)	T81 (T = tied)	76–69–77–72 — 294 (+14)
British Open	T22	75–66–70–70 — 281 (-3) (under par)
Greater Milwaukee Open	T60	67–69–73–68 — 277 (-7)
Bell Canadian Open	11	70–70–68 — 208 (-8)
Quad City Classic	T5	69–64–67–72 — 272 (-8)
B.C. Open	T3	68–66–66 — 200 (-13)
Buick Challenge	WD (withdrew)	
Las Vegas	1st	70–63–68–67–64 — 332 (-27)
La Cantera Texas Open	3rd	69–68–73–67 — 277 (-11)
Disney World/ Oldsmobile Classic	1st	69–63–69–66 — 267 (-21)
THE TOUR Championship	T21	70–78–72–68 — 288 (+8)

Totals for 1996: eleven PGA Events; Tiger ranked twenty-fourth in money earned, and fourteenth in Ryder Cup points.

1997 PGA Results:

Tournament	Round – Final	Total	Winnings	Place
Mercedes Championships	70–67–65–r/o — 202	14–under	$216,000	1st
Phoenix Open	68–68–67–72 — 275	9–under	$20,250	T–18
Pebble Beach ProAm	70–72–63–64 — 269	19–under	$167,200	T–2
Nissan Open	70–70–72–69 — 281	3–under	$14,600	T–20
Bay Hill Invitational	68–71–71–68 — 278	10–under	$42,000	T–9
The Players Championship	71–73–72–73 — 289	1–over	$20,300	T–8
The Masters	70–66–65–64 — 270	18–under	$486,000	1st
Byron Nelson Classic	64–64–67–68 — 263	17–under	$324,000	1st
The Colonial	67–65–64–72 — 268	12–under	$70,400	T–4
The Memorial	72–75–74–r/o — 221	5–over	$3,800	T–8
U.S. Open	74–67–73–72 — 286	6–over	$31,915	T–8
Buick Classic	72–72–71–72 — 287	3–over	$4,568	T–8
British Open	72–74–64–74 — 286	Even	$17,362	T–8
Buick Open	72–68–70–68 — 278	10–under	$43,500	T–8
PGA Championship	70–70–71–75 — 286	6–over	$13,625	T–12
World Series of Golf	67–72–69–70 — 278	2–under	$114,400	T–3
Canadian Open	70–76 — 146	6–over		cut

Walt Disney Classic	66–71–70–71 — 278	10-under	$10,650	T–12
Las Vegas Invitational	68–64–77–71–75 — 355	5-under	$8,663	T–12
Tour Championship	69–68–75–69 — 281	3-under	$97,600	T–12

PGA Tour Events Played: 21
Best Finish: 1st (Mercedes Championships, The Masters, Byron Nelson Classic, and Western Open)
Cuts Made: 20
Top 10 Finishes: 14
Rounds Played: 80
Rounds Under Par: 49
Rounds in the 60s: 35
1997 Earnings: $2,066,833

1998 PGA Results:

Tournament	Round – Final	Total	Winnings	Place
Mercedes Championships	72-67-69-64 — 272	16-under	$149,600	T2
Buick Invitational	71-66-68 — 205	1-under	$109,200	T3
Nissan Open	68-73-65-66 — 272	12-under	$226,800	2nd

Doral-Ryder Open	70–69–71–73 — 283	5–under	$48,000	T9
Bay Hill Invitational	64–70–73–77 — 284	4–under	$37,500	T13
The Players Championship	72–73–73–72 — 290	2–over	$18,886	T35
The Masters	71–72–72–70 — 285	3–under	$89,600	T8
BellSouth Classic	69–67–63–72 — 271	17–under	$324,000	1st
Byron Nelson Classic	65–71–69–67 — 272	8–under	$52,500	T12
The Memorial	70–74–71–73 — 288	Even	$5,148	T51
U.S. Open	74–72–71–73 — 290	10–over	$41,833	T18
Western Open	76–67–69–69 — 281	7–under	$49,225	T9
British Open	65–73–77–66 — 281	Even	$236,250	3rd
Buick Open	71–67–69–68 — 275	13–under	$79,200	T4
PGA Championship	66–72–70–71 — 279	1–under	$69,000	T10
Pebble Beach Pro-Am	76–72 — 148	4–over		W/D
Sprint International	Stableford System	+38	$96,000	4th
World Series of Golf	67–68–70–70 — 275	5–under	$85,500	T5
Nat'l Car Rental Clas.	66–73–68–70 — 277	11–under	$60,250	T7
Tour Championship	75–76–69–69 — 289	9–over	$76,800	20

PGA Tour Events Played: 20
Best Finish: 1st (BellSouth Classic)

Cuts Made: 19
Top 10 Finishes: 13
Rounds Played: 77
Rounds Under Par: 41
Rounds in the 60s: 31
1998 Earnings: $1,841,117

1999 PGA Results:

Tournament	Round – Final	Total	Winnings	Place
Mercedes Champion	69–69–67–72 — 277	15–under	$94,900	T5
Phoenix Open	71–67–70–68 — 276	8–under	$204,000	3rd
Pebble Beach National	72–69–78 — 219	3–over	$6,220	T53
Buick Invitational	68–71–62–65 — 266	22–under	$486,000	1st
Nissan Open	69–68–65–70 — 272	12–under	$209,067	T2
World Golf Championships	Record: 3–1		$150,000	T5
Bay Hill Invitational	74–72–72–72 — 290	2–over	$5,625	T56
The Players Championship	70–71–75–75 — 291	3–over	$107,143	T10
The Masters	72–72–70–75 — 289	1–over	$52,160	T18
MCI Classic	70–70–69–71 — 280	4–under	$28,333	T18

Byron Nelson Classic	61–67–74–69 — 271	9–under	$96,750	T7
The Memorial	68–66–70–69 — 273	15–under	$459,000	1st
U.S. Open	68–71–72–70 — 281	1–over	$196,792	T3
Western Open	68–66–68–71 — 273	15–under	$450,000	1st
British Open	74–72–74–74 — 294	10–over	$82,500	T7
PGA Championship	70–67–68–72 — 277	11–under	$630,000	1st
Sprint International	Stableford System–0	+18	$12,480	T37
World Golf Championship	66–71–62–71 — 270	10–under	$1,000,000	1st
Ryder Cup	Record: 2–3–0			
National Car Rental	66–66–66–73 — 271	17–under	$450,000	1st
The Tour Championship	67–66–67–69 — 269	15–under	$900,000	1st
WGC–American Express	71–69–70–68 — 278	6–under	$1,000,000	1st

PGA Tour Events Played: 22

Best Finish: 1st (Buick Invitational, The Memorial, Western Open, PGA Championship, World Golf Championships–NEC Invitational, National Car Rental Golf Classic, The Tour Championship, WGC–American Express Championship)

Cuts Made: 22

Top 10 Finishes: 16

Rounds Played: 75
Rounds Under Par: 49
Rounds in the 60s: 36
1999 Earnings: $6,620,970

2000 PGA Results:

Tournament	Round – Final	Total	Winnings	Place
Mercedes Championship	71–66–71–68 — 276	16–under	$522,000	1st
Pebble Beach National	68–73–68–64 — 273	15–under	$720,000	1st
Buick Invitational	71–68–67–68 — 274	14–under	$264,000	T2
Nissan Open	68–70–69–72 — 279	5–under	$37,731	T18
World Golf Championship	Record: 5–1		$500,000	2nd
Bay Hill Invitational	69–64–67–70 — 270	18–under	$540,000	1st
The Players Championship	71–71–66–71 — 279	9–under	$648,000	2nd
The Masters	75–72–68–69 — 284	4–under	$165,600	5th
Byron Nelson Classic	73–67–67–63 — 270	10–under	$176,000	T4
The Memorial	71–63–65–70 — 269	19–under	$558,000	1st
U.S. Open	65–69–71–67 — 272	12–under	$800,000	1st
Western Open	70–69–70–72 — 281	7–under	$26,700	T23

British Open	67–66–67–69 — 269	19–under	$759,150	1st
Buick Open	70–70–67–68 — 275	13–under	$57,240	T11
PGA Championship	66–67–70–67 — 270	18–under	$900,000	1st
NEC Invitational	64–61–67–67 — 259	21–under	$1,000,000	1st
Bell Canadian Open	72–65–64–65 — 266	22–under	$594,000	1st

PGA Tour Events Played Through September 2000: 17

Best Finish: 1st (Mercedes Championship, Pebble Beach National, Bay Hill Invitational, The Memorial, U.S. Open, British Open, PGA Championship, NEC Invitational, and Bell Canadian Open)

Cuts Made: 17

Top 10 Finishes: 14

Rounds Played: 64

Rounds Under Par: 58

Rounds in the 60s: 40

2000 Official PGA Tour Earnings Through September: $8,286,821.00

Fan Mail Information:
This address may change at some point, but currently all fan mail may be mailed to Tiger at the following address:

International Management Group
Attn: Tiger Woods
IMG Center Suite #100
1360 East Ninth Street
Cleveland, Ohio 44114-1782

On the World Wide Web, a good place to start is:

http://www.clubtiger.com/

Glossary

Ace: A hole in one is also sometimes called an ace.

Address: This is the stance, or position, a golfer takes right before beginning his or her swing.

AJGA: American Junior Golf Association.

Albatross: Some people describe a double eagle as an albatross. This is when you need three shots *less* than par to finish your hole.

Apron: This is the area of neatly cut grass right around the putting green. The grass on the apron is somewhat longer than the grass on the green.

Back Nine: There are eighteen holes in a round of golf, and the last nine are referred to as the back nine.

Birdie: You score a birdie when you hit one stroke *under* par. In other words, the golfer completes the hole with one less shot than expected.

Bogey: You score a bogey when you hit one stroke *over* par to complete your hole. For example, if the established par for a hole is four shots, a bogey means that it took you *five* shots to hit the ball into the cup.

Bunker: This is a sand pit, or trap, placed on a course intentionally to make the game more challenging.

Caddie: A caddie is the person who accompanies a golfer throughout his or her full round. The caddie carries the golf bag, hands the competitor the proper clubs when asked, provides golf balls, and is just generally available for advice and encouragement. A professional player will usually have a regular caddie.

Casual Water: This is an area of water that was not intentionally placed on the course as a hazard, a puddle, for example. If you hit your ball into casual water, you may move it to one side, and continue without penalty.

Chip Shot: This is a short shot made near the putting green to send the ball up close to the hole, without hitting it too far.

Collar: Sometimes, the apron of short grass around the putting green is called a collar.

Course: This is a grouping of eighteen holes, which comprise a full golf course. Each course is carefully designed to provide as much challenge and enjoyment as possible for the golfer.

Cup: Some people refer to golf holes as cups. This is because of their shape, and the distinctive sound the ball makes when it goes into the hole, as though it were rattling around inside a cup.

Distance Penalty: This is when you are required to hit a new ball from the original location, after being assigned a penalty. For example, if the ball goes out-of-bounds, you must go back and hit a fresh ball, instead of putting the new ball at the spot where the ball went out-of-bounds.

Divot: This is, essentially, a little chunk torn out of the grass by a club. It is considered good manners to replace the divot before you move to the next shot.

Driving Range: This is a place — sometimes right by the course; sometimes not — where golfers go to hit buckets of balls and practice their swings. At a driving range, a golfer will work on his or her technique, as well as hitting for distance. A driving range is the golfing equivalent of a baseball batting cage.

Double Bogey: This is when a player needs *two* extra shots over par in order to complete a hole. For example, if the par value for a hole is five shots, and you need seven shots to hit the ball in the cup, you have scored a double bogey.

Double Eagle: You score a double eagle — or an albatross — when you shoot *three* strokes under par.

Eagle: An eagle is when you are able to complete a hole in *two* strokes under par.

Fairway: This is the huge grassy area of the hole before you get to the much smoother grass of the putting green. The bulk of a golf course consists of its eighteen fairways. The putting greens and tee-off areas are much smaller.

Fat Shot: When you make a fat shot, that means you struck the turf accidentally with your club before hitting the ball. When this happens, you will generally lose both the control and distance on your shot.

Flagstick: This is a small flag placed on top of a pole in the middle of each hole. That way, a player can see exactly where the hole is from hundreds of yards away, and be able to aim toward it. Once a player is on the putting green, the flagstick is removed from the hole, so that the player can putt without any distractions.

Fore: This is what players — or caddies — traditionally shout right before making a shot. That way, observers and other players will know that a ball is coming and be able to get out of the way.

Fringe: This is another word for the apron, or collar, that abuts the putting area.

Front Nine: This is what players called the first nine holes of an eighteen-round game.

Grain: No matter how well-manicured a putting green is, grass tends to grow at an angle. This is called the grain. Hitting *with* the grain is considered easier, because it is much smoother. Hitting *against* the grain means that the ball's movements may be less easy to predict.

Green: This is also known as the putting green, and it is the area of extremely short-cut grass surrounding the hole.

Green Fee: This is the price you have to pay the golf club, in order to play a round of golf. Golf is a very expensive game, and green fees are often quite high. Maintenance costs are very high on golf courses, and these expenses are passed along to the golfers themselves.

Hacker: This is a disparaging term, referring to a person who is a lousy golfer. The word *hack* implies mediocrity in all areas of life, but originally, it began as a golf phrase.

Handicap: Depending on the numbers of shots you usually shoot above par after completing a full eighteen holes, your average — or handicap — as a golfer is established. By using handicaps, golfers of very different abilities can play together and enjoy themselves. For example, let's say that par for a given course is 70, and you have a +15 handicap. If you shoot an 85, you have shot par for your eighteen holes. Therefore, if you are playing someone with a +5 handicap, he or she would need to shoot at least 75 in order to tie you. If he or she scores anything less than 75, you lose. If he or she scores more than 75, you win. Handicaps were created to allow people with different levels of skill to compete equally.

Hazard: This is an obstruction placed anywhere on the course to make the game more interesting.

Hole: There are eighteen holes on a golf course. Each hole is approximately four inches wide and four inches deep.

Hole in One: This means that you have miraculously managed to hit the ball hundreds of yards from your original tee directly into the hole.

Honor: Since golfers play in pairs, or foursomes, the honor is the person, or team, who gets to shoot first. On the first tee, when there is no score yet, this would usually be decided by flipping a coin, or something of that nature. After that, the person, or team, who has the best score at any given time, has the honor of hitting first. Sometimes, the person who had the lowest score on the previous hole is given the honor of shooting first at the next hole.

Irons: These are golf clubs with metal heads, the front of which are slanted and wedge-shaped. Traditionally, a player has nine irons. The lower numbered clubs are heavier and longer, and will hit the ball a greater distance.

Irregular Lie: This is when you have hit the ball from a funny position. For example, if you hit your ball nicely up the fairway and it lands comfortably in the grass, you have an easy lie. But, if it lands behind a tree that you have to try and hit the ball *around*, or under a bench or something, then you have to hit from an irregular lie.

Kiltie: This is the leather flap on top of a golf shoe.

Knee-Knocker: This is a short putt of maybe four to five feet, which is close enough so that it should go in, but just far enough away to make the player feel nervous; so, theoretically, his or her knees will knock together.

Lay-up Shot: This is a strategic choice a golfer may make to avoid an obstruction on the course. For example, if there is a large bunker between the golfer and the hole, the golfer might not be sure if he or she can hit the ball *over* the obstruction. So, to play it safe, the golfer will hit a short shot right in front of the obstruction. Then, with his or her next shot, it will be easy to hit the ball safely over the obstruction and avoid getting penalized. This is a conservative strategy, but often a wise one. You take an extra shot by doing this, but you avoid risking a major mistake.

Lie: This is the position where your ball lands. There are all sorts of lies — irregular lies, downhill lies, etc. — each of which describes a different situation.

Links: This describes a particular kind of golf course, which was designed directly by the ocean. These courses are the types that were used in golf's early days in Scotland, and many players love the traditional aspects of playing links.

Loose Impediments: These are objects like leaves, rocks, and tiny sticks, which were not intentionally placed on a

161

golf course. If a loose impediment is blocking a player's ball, she or he can remove it without penalty.

Lost Ball: Since each golf hole is usually several hundreds of yards long, sometimes you lose sight of your ball after you hit it. If the ball can not be found after five minutes of searching, usually a new ball will be placed in the spot where you *think* your ball probably should have landed. You are penalized one stroke for this.

LPGA: Ladies Professional Golf Association.

Match Play: This is when two players, or two teams, play a match against each other. The player, or team, who wins the most *holes*, wins the match.

Medal Play: This is the format used in most professional tournaments. The player is not scored on the basis of how many holes he or she wins, but how many strokes he or she takes to complete the full eighteen holes. In a major tournament, several rounds will be played, and the scores from each day are added up. At the end, the player with the lowest score is the winner.

Obstruction: In contrast to a hazard, which has been placed intentionally on the golf course, an obstruction is something that is on the course, but shouldn't be.

Open Tournament: In an open tournament, amateur players are allowed to compete with professionals. In order to remain an amateur, however, a player cannot accept money or other benefits. As soon as a player gets paid, he or she is considered a professional.

Out-of-bounds: Each hole is designed to fit within a certain area, and if your shot goes out of this area, you have hit the ball out-of-bounds.

Par: This is the established number of shots that it should take a skilled player to complete any one hole, from start to finish. Par usually consists of three to five shots, although it varies depending on the golf course in question.

Penalty Strokes: As explained above, players are penalized one stroke whenever they hit a ball out-of-bounds. A player

is also penalized if he or she hits the ball into a water hazard.

PGA: Professional Golfers' Association.

Pin: Another name for the flagstick.

Pitch Shot: This is a short shot — usually less than one hundred yards — during which the ball stays in the air almost the entire time. When it lands, it sometimes bounces, but it will rarely roll much.

Pitching Wedge: This is the special club used to knock your ball out of a bunker, or to make short shots near the green.

Play Through: Sometimes, on a crowded golf course, different sets of players bunch up together. This is the golf version of a traffic jam. If one set of players is playing very quickly, the other players will usually let them go on ahead, or "play through."

Preshot Routine: All good players have a preshot routine, or ritual. These are the steps a player takes before *every single shot*. A skilled player will never change this routine, in order to help keep his or her game consistent. For example, if you usually look down once, look up, and look down again before taking your shot, you should *always* do that in competition.

Provisional Ball: If you lose your ball, or hit it out-of-bounds or into a water hazard, the game is not over. Instead, a new — or provisional — ball is placed at the general spot where your ball appeared to land, or where it first went out-of-bounds. You are penalized one stroke, but are able to continue your round.

Putter: This is the golf club you use on the putting green, to tap the ball into the hole. A putter is used for the final shot (or shots), which requires precision, delicacy, and control.

Putting Green: This is the small grassy area directly surrounding the hole. It is mowed very closely, and is so smooth that it is almost like hitting on a carpet.

Rough: Golf courses are normally kept in beautiful condition, with smooth, manicured grass. But, in order to give the game some variety, the outside edges of any given hole are usually left unmowed, or *rough*.

Sand Wedge: This is a club with a very sharply angled wedge, which is used to loft one's ball out of bunkers.

Scratch Player: This is a very skillful player, who is likely to play any given course with a score of par.

Shank: This is when you try and hit the ball straight ahead — but for some reason, your swing is off, and the ball goes flying wildly to one side.

Slice: This is when you try to hit the ball forward, but it veers off and curves away to the side. When you slice the ball, it sails ahead and off to the side, instead of landing exactly where you wanted it to land. An experienced golfer might *intentionally* slice his or her shot, in order to get around an obstruction of some kind.

Stroke: This is any intentional forward swing of your golf club in an attempt to hit the ball.

Stroke Play: This is just another word for medal play, which is the form of scoring used in most tournaments.

Tee: This is the little wooden or plastic holder for the ball. When the ball is sitting on top of a tee, it is slightly raised from the ground, so you should be able to hit it without slamming your club into the grass and creating a divot.

Tee Area: This is the small grassy section at the very beginning of each hole, where a golfer takes his or her first shot.

Tee Off: This is the term for actually swinging and hitting your first shot.

Tee Time: This is the time at which you are scheduled to begin your golf game. Missing, or being late, for your tee time is considered very rude.

Topping: This is when your swing is faulty, and you swing over the top of the ball, instead of getting underneath the ball and lifting it into a drive. When you top a ball, you are essentially driving it straight into the ground, instead of sending it forward.

Triple Bogey: This is when you need *three* extra shots above par in order to complete your hole.

USGA: United States Golf Association. It sets the rules and regulations for the game of golf in the United States.

Waggle: Many golfers swing their clubs back and forth slightly, trying to get a rhythm, before breaking into their full swing. This little warm-up ritual is called a waggle. Some players, instead of moving their clubs, will move their hips, instead. Other players would do both. In any case, the individual waggle is part of most players' preshot routines.

Woods: These are the heavy, powerful clubs used for teeing off. A player always selects a wood to get a lot of distance on the ball. Woods used to be *made* of wood, but today, most of them are actually manufactured from metal, graphite, and other substances. Like irons, the lower the number, the more powerful the club is.

Some Web Sites
You Might Enjoy Exploring

1. http://www.pga.com/
2. http://www.lpga.com/
3. http://www.usga.org/
4. http://www.golfweb.com/
5. http://www.iGolf.com/
6. http://www.kidsgolf.com/
7. http://www.chipmunk.com/
8. http://www.golf.com/
9. http://www.greatgolf.com/

Remember, Web addresses change frequently, and some of these may already be outdated.